Changing v
retirement

Changing work and retirement

SOCIAL POLICY AND
THE OLDER WORKER

FRANK LACZKO and
CHRIS PHILLIPSON

Open University Press
MILTON KEYNES · PHILADELPHIA

Open University Press
Celtic Court
22 Ballmoor
Buckingham
MK18 1XW

and

1900 Frost Road, Suite 101
Bristol, PA 19007, US

First Published 1991

Copyright © Frank Laczko and Chris Phillipson 1991

British Library Cataloguing in Publication Data

Laczko, Frank
  Changing work and retirement: Social policy and
  the older worker.
  I. Title.   II. Phillipson, Chris
  306.3

  ISBN 0–335–09931–9
  ISBN 0–335–09930–0 pbk

Library of Congress Cataloging-in-Publication Data

  Laczko, Frank, 1957–
  Changing work and retirement: social policy and the older worker
  Frank Laczko, Chris Phillipson.
      p.   cm.
  Includes bibliographical references and index.
  ISBN 0–335–09931–9. – ISBN 0–335–09930–0 (pbk.)
  1. Aged – Employment – Great Britain.   2. Age and employment – Great
Britain.   3. Labor market – Great Britain.   4. Early retirement –
Great Britain.   I. Phillipson, Chris.   II. Title.
HD6283.G7L33   1991
331.3′98′0941 – dc20
                                                                          91–2507
                                                                          CIP

Typeset by Type Study, Scarborough
Printed and bound in Great Britain by
Woolnough Bookbinding, Irthlingborough

To Florence and Jane

Contents

List of tables

Acknowledgements

The authors of this book were fortunate enough to be invited, in 1987, to join a small group of researchers to work on cross-national developments in the field of retirement. Some of the ideas and findings reviewed in this study draw upon discussions and perspectives developed at early meetings with these researchers. We are especially grateful to Martin Rein and Martin Kohli for the original invitation to join the group. Frank Laczko would like to acknowledge the ESRC for the award of two grants with which he was associated for studies of data from the *General Household Survey* and *Labour Force Survey*. This work is reflected in a number of the chapters in this book. The authors are also grateful to John Skelton of the Open University Press for his consistent support. Carolyn Medd was extremely helpful in guiding the manuscript through to publication. The final typescript of the book was prepared by Sue Allingham who undertook this task with considerable care and efficiency.

1

Introduction: between work and retirement

This book is concerned with one of the major social trends in Britain in the last two decades – the sharp fall in the proportion of older people in paid employment. This trend has been especially marked among men aged 55–64, with over half of men aged 60–64 and one third of men aged 55–59 no longer in paid employment. The changes in employment are part of an international trend, with the majority of industrialized countries experiencing dramatic falls in labour participation rates (see Table 1.1). This development is even more remarkable when one considers that retirement is a relatively recent social phenomenon, and that throughout the nineteenth century and well into the twentieth, the majority of older people did not retire (Myles 1984).

At the same time, there has been a significant increase in life expectancy in Britain. In 1991 a 65-year-old man can expect to live 13.4 more years, and a woman of 65 can expect to live 17.3 more years. A century earlier, a man and woman of the same age could expect to live a further 10.3 years and 11.3 years respectively. Although there are still substantial class differences in life expectancy, this means that many people who leave work early can expect to spend a substantial proportion of their lives, possibly twenty to thirty years, outside of the paid work-force. Indeed, for some people this phase of their life may be almost as long as their working lives, and often longer than their childhood.

Until the late 1980s public policy in Britain, as in most other advanced industrialized countries, was largely in favour of encouraging older people to leave work early in order to reduce unemployment. Unemployment was primarily defined as a problem of youth unemployment, even though older workers once unemployed face the longest average duration of unemployment of any age group (OECD 1988a). However, as a result of economic considerations – long-term

Table 1.1   Labour force participation rates for men aged 55–59, 60–64 and 65 plus in selected OECD countries

Men aged 55–59

	1965	1970	1975	1980	1985	1988
France	82.9	82.9	83.3	80.9	67.8	67.3
Germany	90.5	88.4	84.5	80.0	76.2	76.6
Japan	90.0	91.2	92.2	91.2	90.3	91.3
Netherlands	–	–	78.9	74.8	64.8	60.0
Sweden	92.8	90.8	89.7	87.7	87.6	85.9
UK	95.7	95.3	93.0	90.1	81.8	81.6
USA	85.7	88.3	83.3	80.9	78.9	78.7

Men aged 60–64

	1965	1970	1975	1980	1985	1988
France	68.8	68.0	56.7	47.6	30.8	25.4
Germany	78.1	71.8	56.2	42.5	32.4	31.5
Japan	82.8	81.5	79.4	77.8	72.5	71.1
Netherlands	–	–	64.9	48.8	27.8	14.6
Sweden	83.0	79.5	74.0	69.0	65.1	64.1
UK	89.2	86.7	82.3	71.2	54.5	55.1
USA	79.2	71.7	64.5	59.8	55.1	53.8

Men aged 65 and over

	1965	1970	1975	1980	1985	1988
France	28.3	19.5	13.9	7.5	5.3	4.6
Germany	24.0	17.2	10.8	7.0	5.1	4.7
Japan	56.3	49.4	44.4	41.0	37.0	35.8
Netherlands	–	–	8.0	4.8	3.5	2.8
Sweden	37.7	28.9	19.9	14.2	11.0	19.0
UK	23.7	20.1	15.6	10.3	8.2	7.7
USA	26.6	25.7	20.7	18.3	15.2	15.9

Source: Adapted from OECD Labour Force Statistics, Paris 1984/1989

concerns about the cost of an ageing population and short-term concerns about the decline in the number of young people entering the labour force – public policy is beginning to change. Older workers are now being encouraged, in some cases, to delay their retirement.

This development has increased the uncertainty for many of those faced with the possibility of leaving work ahead of state retirement age.

The future of work and retirement

This book aims, first of all, to assess the factors contributing to the sharp decline in employment among older workers. It then seeks to analyse variations in early retirement, particularly in respect of social class and gender. The book also examines the policy issues surrounding changes in work patterns, setting out an agenda for change in the 1990s. Finally, the study examines the nature of early retirement from a theoretical standpoint, linking changes in the labour market to the reconstruction of middle and old age. These specific aims are located, first, within a theoretical perspective drawn from the field of social gerontology; second, a reappraisal of the definition of early retirement. We shall now summarize some of the key points raised by the approach taken in this book, before providing a plan of the study and a review of the data sources from which many of the arguments are derived.

The political economy of old age

An influential perspective in gerontology in the 1980s has been that of the political economy of ageing (Estes *et al.* 1982; Phillipson 1982). This approach has been used in recent years not only to interpret the position of elderly people in advanced industrialized societies, but also to explain the emergence of retirement. The political economy model focuses on the way in which retirement is shaped by the social structure and by the social and economic factors which affect the individual's place in that structure (Stone and Minkler 1984). This approach highlights the impact of social class, gender and race on the experience of retirement. In short, retirement is seen as 'socially constructed', varying according to lifelong social status and prevailing state policies (Phillipson and Walker 1986). This theoretical argument, along with others, has been important in shifting the focus of investigation in social gerontology from that of asking how individuals have adjusted to retirement to examining the socio-political factors which influence retirement outcomes (Estes *et al.* 1982).

Another argument from political economy suggests that during the twentieth century, society has deliberately promoted the marginalization and dependency of elderly people, and that the state has played a major role in this process (Townsend 1986). According to this viewpoint, the history of retirement can be interpreted primarily as an 'age discriminatory social process designed to exclude older people *en masse* from the workforce' (Walker 1990: 59). It is also argued that by having to retire from gainful work, older people are forced into a position of heightened dependency arising from the loss of income and status associated with employment (Townsend 1986). Critics of this view argue, first, that it places too much emphasis on the role of demand factors in explaining the growth of retirement; second, that it implies that people in employment are less dependent than those in retirement. An alternative view has been put forward by Paul Johnson (1989a), where he challenges the 'automatic association of retirement with dependency, and of work with independence' (Johnson 1989a: 66). He goes on to argue that

It is certainly true that employment opportunities for men have declined sharply over the last eighty years but it is far from clear that this has been solely due to a contraction of demand for them. Improved economic status now gives more elderly people the option of a fairly comfortable retirement which they may prefer to continued employment in unattractive work.

(Johnson 1989a: 71)

And Martin Kohli has added to the debate with the observation that

It is true that where the pension is very low compared to work incomes, the measure of independence that it provides may be slight. . . . But those among the elderly who receive low pensions are typically also those – as the structured dependency authors themselves make clear – who have experienced precarious and low-paid employment careers, i.e. have had particularly little control over the risks of the labour market. For them, retirement means rather more security and control over their incomes, and certainly less dependency on the relational level.

(Kohli 1988: 377)

One of the aims of this book is to examine retirement trends within the context of these contrasting theoretical perspectives. In particular, we shall suggest that both perspectives have major limitations within the context of changes within the labour market in the 1970s and 1980s. We shall show that many older workers have been pushed out of the labour force, not into a secure retirement, but into long-term unemployment or into forms of non-employment such as long-term disability. Therefore, in some senses, the debate about 'voluntary' or 'involuntary' retirement is somewhat redundant; retirement, in its traditional form, is experienced by fewer and fewer workers. Retirement in the 1990s has evolved new patterns and social attitudes. These developments represent a challenge both to existing theories in social gerontology and, at a wider level, are raising major social questions both for older people and for society generally.

Early exit, old age and the meaning of retirement

One of the main arguments of this book is that we have entered *a new period in the history of retirement*. An intermediary phase has emerged between the end of employment and receipt of a state pension. The transition between work and retirement has changed and has become more complex in recent years. In the 1980s there was an increase both in the range of pre-retirement categories and statuses as well as an increase in the number of older persons entering these positions. At the same time, the public pension system does not play the same role as it once did in defining the beginning of retirement and old age (Guillemard 1989). These changes have affected the way in which retirement is defined both by society and the individuals affected. This is especially the case with the phenomenon of early retirement, the meaning of which has undergone radical change since the 1970s. There are many ways of defining retirement and early retirement and no single definition can be used unambiguously. The official definition used in government information to older people is that

> Early retirement means retirement before state pensionable age. You may, for example, have been made redundant late in your working life and feel that there is little point in looking for another job. Or you may have been working in an occupation with an occupational pension age below state pensionable age – like the Civil Service or Armed Forces.
>
> (DSS 1990: 9)

However, as Bond points out there can be many other definitions of retirement:

> many studies utilise administrative definitions such as time of retirement or age at retirement; others construct normative definitions based on the researcher's perceptions of retirement such as the number of hours worked per week or the number of years of employment; and some studies use the individual's own perception of whether they were retired or not.
>
> (Bond 1986: 221)

Whatever definition is used, we believe that there are good reasons for distinguishing between *early exit* from employment and *early retirement*, to describe the way in which older people have been leaving the labour force in recent years. Thus, it is misleading to view the fall in activity rates simply as part of a trend towards earlier retirement. Retirement, as it is traditionally defined, is seen to come at a fixed age and accompanied by a pension provided by the state. In other words, retirement is taken at a predicted stage in the life course and reflects relatively long-standing societal norms (Casey and Laczko 1989). However, as we shall demonstrate in this book, the retirement of many older people in recent years has not in fact come at a predictable stage in the life course; nor at an age which has established itself as a norm for society. Moreover, many people, who are now generally considered to be retired, do not receive a public pension and do not even consider themselves to be retired. There is, in fact, much ambiguity in the status of older people, who find themselves in an intermediary phase between employment and retirement. This situation, we argue, itself reflects the ambiguity in public policy towards older people.

Distinguishing between early exit and early retirement is helpful for other reasons. Early retirement has, in some instances, been used to legitimize the exclusion of older people from the labour force. One of the reasons why there has been less public concern about the circumstances of the older long-term unemployed is because they are considered to have available to them the 'alternative role' of early retiree. Early retirement is a term used by unions, employers and governments to justify the effective dismissal of older people, and to shift a disproportionate burden of unemployment on to older members of the labour force. Use of the term 'early exit' thus raises the issue of the problems faced by *some* groups of workers who are situated in between work and retirement. The social policy implications of the difficulties faced by such groups is a central concern of this book.

Another advantage in using the term early exit is that it focuses on *differences* within the population of older workers. For example there is the likelihood of greater inequality in retirement arising from the varied routes which people take out of the work-force. As we shall show in Chapter 5 there is a close link between early exit and poverty in Britain, possibly more so than in other EC countries (Laczko 1990). At a time when the income position of older people in general is said to be improving, there is a danger that early exit is creating a new category of poverty among the retired (OECD 1989). Our analysis also suggests that the intermediary phase which has emerged between employment and retirement is unlikely to disappear in the short term. The social consequences of early exit are likely to be long term.

Unemployment has been falling more slowly among older people than other groups in the labour force. Current official projections of activity rates up to the year 2000 are that participation rates will fall further for men over 60 and will show little change for men aged 55–59 and for female workers (Bosanquet *et al.* 1990).

However, work and retirement after 50 are likely to be characterized by greater flexibility. This is because the labour market for older workers has changed radically since 1979 (Casey and Laczko 1991). It is now increasingly dominated by self-employed people, part-time workers and female employees. In policy terms, there is the debate about the decade of retirement and the use of a partial retirement scheme similar to that adopted in Sweden. All these developments confirm the variety of changes running through the life course, especially from the period of mid-life and early old age. The aim of this book is to provide both a detailed analysis of these changes and to consider some alternative policies that might be developed for older workers.

Data

Many of the data that are used in this study come from analysis of the Labour Force Surveys (LFS) and the General Household Surveys (GHS). We have used data from various years in the 1980s, including 1980–3 and 1986. Both these surveys have the advantage of being nationally representative, which is especially important since the last representative survey of retirement was based on a sample of people interviewed in 1977 (Parker 1980). Given that it is becoming increasingly difficult for British social scientists to carry out their own large-scale surveys, data-sets such as the GHS and LFS provide the only feasible way of obtaining a nationally representative sample (Dale *et al.* 1988: 26). Although data-sets such as the LFS and GHS have not been specifically designed to provide information on retirement, they none the less provide a rich source of data on this subject. The GHS is a national sample survey of the general population resident in private (that is non-institutional) households which has been conducted continuously since 1971. It is based on interviews with about 10,000 households (25,000 individuals) per year. Prior to 1982 the achieved sample size was somewhat larger, about 12,000 households. The GHS data are collected from two interview schedules. The Household Schedule covers topics such as housing tenure, consumer durables and migration, and is answered by one adult member of the household, usually the head or his spouse (the definition of head of household used by the GHS means that heads of households are generally men). Each household member aged 16 and over answers an Individual Schedule about their employment, job satisfaction, educational attainment, health and use of health services, and income. In addition, topics such as leisure, smoking, drinking, family planning and the circumstances of elderly people are included in some years (Dale *et al.* 1988: 62).

The LFS has a much larger sample size than the GHS. It is based on 0.5 per cent sample and collects information from about 80,000 households and about 120,000 people each year. Information about the labour market activity of each adult aged 16 and over in sample households is collected. The LFS provides the most comprehensive picture of the British labour market. Unlike the GHS, however, the LFS provides virtually no information on income. The surveys can therefore be used to complement each other, as the GHS sample size is often too small to analyse certain variables relating to small sub-groups of the population. Both the GHS and the LFS have a high response rate of about 82–5 per cent (Dale *et al.* 1988: 25).

One particular weakness with most research on retirement is that the data used have been cross-sectional, collected at only one point in time. One advantage of using the LFS is that information is collected on labour market activity one year before the survey. This makes it possible to compare people's circumstances before and after they have left employment.

Plan of the book

We begin in Chapter 2 with an examination of the historical context behind the development of retirement in the twentieth century. This chapter also outlines the rapid growth in early exit/retirement in the 1970s and 1980s. Chapter 3 focuses on age discrimination in the labour market, highlighting the attitudes of both government and employers. An attempt is made to analyse older workers' exclusion from the labour market from a theoretical perspective, using dual labour market theory, and the theory of the reserve army of labour. The chapter ends by locating the development of early exit within the context of moves towards more flexible work regimes and labour contracts.

Chapter 4 provides an analysis of the way in which early exit has developed in Britain in the absence of major public provision for early retirement. We outline the ways in which people have been leaving the labour force early and the benefits that they receive. Using data from Britain and other countries, we look at whether people who have left employment early define themselves as retired. The chapter concludes with a discussion of the changing meaning and significance of retirement.

Chapter 5 reviews some of the reasons given by individuals for leaving employment before state retirement age; the aim here is to provide a better understanding of the process of retirement. We are particularly concerned in this chapter to examine what evidence there is in support of the view that older workers have been leaving the labour force involuntarily. Particular attention is given to gender differences in routes out of paid employment. In the final part of the chapter we examine the extent to which early exit is associated with low income, and what might be the long-term financial consequences of early exit for older people.

Chapter 6 examines the implications of current patterns of early exit from the labour force for employers and the labour market. The chapter assesses the advantages and disadvantages for firms that use early retirement. Next the broader impact of early exit is examined, in particular its impact on employment. Finally we try to assess how far enterprises are likely to be prepared to respond favourably to incentives from the state to retain or employ more older workers, rather than encouraging further early exit.

Chapter 7 is concerned with the politics of early exit. We are interested, in particular, in identifying the reasons behind the consensus in favour of early retirement, together with the reaction to this consensus. The chapter assesses the debate that took place between government, employers, unions and others during the 1970s and 1980s concerning both the age of retirement and flexible retirement. We also examine the beginning of a discussion about possible conflict between generations over the allocation of welfare and related benefits. An assessment is also made of the impact on retirement policy of this debate.

In chapter 8, drawing on evidence from earlier chapters, we suggest alternative policies for the future in areas such as employment, pensions and continuing education. Finally, Chapter 9 sets many of the arguments within a sociological framework, identifying new social arrangements which will need to be developed to support workers facing a period of transition between work and retirement.

2

Retirement and early exit

Introduction

Old age has emerged as an issue characterized by two distinctive features: first, the growth in the proportion of the population aged 60–65 and over; second, the withdrawal of older people (men especially) from the labour market. In Britain in the 1880s, nearly three-quarters of men aged 65+ were still in employment; by the early 1950s this had fallen to one-third; and by 1990 just 3 per cent of men were actually employed full-time (the figure for women was 1 per cent). By 1985 there was only a 50:50 chance of a man aged 60–64 having a job, let alone a full-time job. Hundreds and thousands of people in this age range, who had expected to work until retirement, found themselves with no work and ineligible for a state pension.

In this study the main focus will be on the acceleration of early exit from work in the 1970s and 1980. However, while it is clear that high unemployment levels are a major explanation for this development, the causal factors behind long-term retirement trends still need to be unravelled. The focus of this chapter is, first, to provide a brief historical review of some of the elements influencing the emergence of retirement. Second, to summarize the pattern of early exit among men and women in the 1970s and 1980s. Finally, the chapter will conclude with some general observations about the development of retirement within capitalist economies, drawing upon a number of theoretical and empirical studies.

The emergence of retirement

Historical and sociological studies of retirement have substantially revised our views about how we see the development of this important social and economic institution. In the 1960s and 1970s functionalist theory and modernization theory emphasized the marginalization of older people in the shift from a rural to an industrial economy (Parsons 1942; Burgess 1960; Cowgill and Holmes 1972). The key features of industrialization producing this effect were held to be the introduction of new technology, the impact of urbanization, and the importance attached to education and social mobility. These factors, it was argued, set up a chain reaction which lowered the status of older people. The key issues were seen in terms of first, the fact that age itself was no longer held in the same regard as in traditional society; second, new technology reduced the value placed upon the skills of older workers; third, migration and urbanization led to the break-up of the extended family; finally, the growth of education was seen to undermine the role of older people as purveyors of skills and knowledge. Taking all of these changes together, the position of retirement was portrayed in terms of a 'roleless role' (Burgess 1960), with the possibility of considerable stress arising in the period of transition after work (Cooper et al. 1988).

This particular model has, however, been the subject of considerable criticism, both from sociologists and historians working in the field of old age. Richard Smith (1984), for example, argues that the 'structured dependence' of older people is exclusive neither to the twentieth century nor to industrialization. He suggests, in fact, that one must recognize 'a long series of endeavours to resolve persistent questions concerning the duties of the individual, the family and the community for the provision of the less fortunate'. Research by historians of the family indicates that there has been no 'binding cultural norm' that older people would be cared for within the family group (Robin 1984). Indeed, the very existence of elaborate retirement contracts, whereby retirees exchanged their land and buildings for specific services and support, indicates the tension between generations; the contract itself leaving very little to chance in respect of the provision of food, clothing and shelter (Hanawalt 1986). And social anthropologists have pointed to the complexity of the experience of old age in all types of societies, with status being influenced by factors such as class, wealth, culture and family support (Sokolovsky 1983; Foner 1984).

In addition, as Blaikie and Macnicol (1986) observe, the process of marginalization may not have been exclusive to older people. They suggest that

It may simply have been part of a wider process of classification that was being applied to other age groups in society (for example, children, the unemployed, the mentally retarded) – a consequence of a more specialised division of labour and an increasingly interventionist state with better techniques of classification, identification and surveillance.

(Blaikie and Macnicol 1986: 96;
see also Haber 1978; Armstrong 1983)

But even if we reject a simple model of older people being marginalized in the move from a rural to an industrial economy, it is clear that a form of structured dependence did eventually emerge, in which the imposition of compulsory retirement played a significant part (Townsend 1981). At the same time, a point that needs to be stressed is that while retirement has always been part of economic and social custom, its twentieth-century form must be regarded as fundamentally different in scale and the type of relationships involved (Phillipson 1982). We can agree here with Smith (1984) and Thomas (1976) that forms of retirement have probably existed throughout history; indeed, retirement has been seen as a functional necessity where work is in short or fluctuating supply (Thomas 1976). There is little doubt, as well, that the implications of losing work could arouse genuine fear. According to Keith Thomas

For most manual workers old age meant, first, a move to lighter (and lower-paid) work, then a decline to abject dependence. Every contemporary list of paupers contains a proportion described as 'ancient and decrepit', 'aged and past work', 'old and her work done'. For miners, tailors, and metal-workers this stage could come very quickly. Almshouses did not take those capable of working, yet the minimum age of admission was sometimes as low as forty. For literary commentators fifty was usually the point when old age began: 'at fifty', said Bishop Babington, 'we go down the hill again and every day grow weaker and weaker'. When old age pensions were first proposed, by Defoe in the 1690s, and by Dowdeswell in 1772, fifty was the age at which they were to be payable. On this point Burke agreed with Paine: from the age of fifty a workman's decline became 'every year more sensible'.

(Thomas 1976: 240; see also Stearns 1975)

On the other hand, for the more prosperous middle class, there has been a desire to leave work once the raising of a family has been complete. In the nineteenth century, for example, Davidoff and Hall note that

Once the effort of raising, educating and placing their numerous offspring was well underway, many middle-class men seem to have either withdrawn from active business or professional practice to take up a different occupation, to take part in political, scientific or voluntary affairs or to give more attention to serious religious concerns. Any or none of these might be combined with simply enjoying their homes and gardens. Whatever their motivation, such withdrawal gave scope to the younger men in the enterprise to take over greater responsibility. Archibald Kenrick's nephew John wrote to him when the older man was considering changing the partnership agreements in order to gradually withdraw from the firm.

The prospect of such a season of leisure towards the decline of life, is one of the strongest motives to a man to go steadily on year after year with the drudgery of business; indeed without it, the complete absorption of many men's minds in the affairs of the world in the early and middle part of life would be hardly justifiable.

(Davidoff and Hall 1987: 225)

But the experience of retirement in the twentieth century (and particularly from the 1960s onwards) is somewhat different, either to the experience of decrepitude or individual leisure achieved through the successful pursuit of the work ethic. What makes it different is that people increasingly experience retirement both as a social institution *and* as a distinctive stage in the life course (Atchley 1988; Fennell *et al.* 1988). To illustrate this point, we shall now examine the emergence of retirement in the twentieth century, focusing initially on findings from British and American research.

Retirement in the twentieth century

Modern retirement policy is a product of the late nineteenth century as large private companies and branches of the civil service adopted pension policies for their employees. Hannah (1986) observes that prior to this, the practice of fixed retirement ages was somewhat rare, with many of the very early pension schemes taking a flexible approach as regards retirement age. By the turn of the century, however, mandatory retirement was becoming increasingly common (Graebner 1980). The earliest examples of widespread enforcement of this were, in the case of Britain, for clerical and administrative employees in areas such as the civil service and banks. In the USA pension systems, along with mandatory retirement, were first adopted by the railroad companies. Haber (1978) suggests that this was hardly accidental:

In the late nineteenth century, transportation executives confronted the best organised and most powerful brotherhood of workers. These unions demonstrated their strength by calling for strikes that paralysed the nation's business. Facing with the growing power of labour, and troubled by a highly unstable workforce, the managers in this industry adopted paternalistic welfare programmes, hopeful that they would pacify their disruptive employees.

(Haber 1978: 81–2)

The reasons for the spread of mandatory retirement will be summarized at the end of this chapter, but two points might be made to indicate some of the pressures on both employers and employees. First, Graebner (1980) observes the development of a view in the late nineteenth and early twentieth century, that an economy which offered jobs to 'inefficient' workers (such as the old) could not be regarded as functioning properly. The image here was of the 'worn out' worker who needed to be pensioned-off rather than retained in the labour force, if efficiency was to be maintained. As E.G. McDonald (1928) put it, in an article in the journal *Factory and Industrial Management*: 'Today even our biggest executives are employees, and business management has come to realize that a businesslike procedure demands that the human element in any business be depreciated year by year precisely as plant and equipment are depreciated' (McDonald 1928: 536). Second, and running alongside this view, was acceptance of the idea that retirement would be an effective measure in combating unemployment among the young. Here, in fact, was the basis for age discrimination: the old, it was suggested, would suffer less from the absence of a job; their social needs were less, and, more importantly for the state, they were unlikely to rebel at being denied work (Graebner 1980). Carole Haber (1978) summarizes these points:

> Enforced retirement also reflected widely held notions about the abilities of the aged. The same set of beliefs that had segregated the elderly into old age homes and almshouses now restricted their right to employment. Basic to every aspect of the pension system was a conception of the old as incapacitated, inefficient, and, above all, the powerless sector of society. To some degree, this characterisation had a factual basis; the unemployed aged who were forced to seek refuge in institutions certainly did benefit from the pension system. In addition, many elderly people gladly accepted their years of leisure. But they did not leave the work force merely because they had grown old. The restrictions that limited the employment of the elderly were consciously devised in an attempt to regulate the labour market.

As a result, in the late 19th century, mandatory retirement first developed into a new, economically determined and culturally-legitimated stage of existence.

(Haber 1978: 89)

Older people and the depression

The product of these trends was an economy which provided a diminishing pool of opportunities to older workers – especially when they had reached their sixties. Studies of unemployment in Lancashire (Chapman and Hallsworth 1909), York (Rowntree and Lasker 1911) and West Yorkshire (Richardson 1936), all indicated the difficulties faced by the unskilled and semi-skilled in particular, from the age of 40 onwards. Rowntree and Lasker found that

> It is unfortunately indisputable that when an unskilled worker gets past 40 he finds it very difficult to meet with an employer who is willing to give him regular work. He may be able to work quite well as a younger man, but in a labour market where the supply of unskilled labour almost invariably exceeds the demand, an employer having to choose between a younger and an older man not unnaturally chooses the younger.
>
> (Rowntree and Lasker 1911: 53)

The economic depression in the 1930s had a particularly severe effect on older workers. Thus while in 1927 one in every eleven insured men aged 18–24 was unemployed, with the proportion of those over 55 being one in seven; ten years later the proportion of the former had stayed the same, while that of the latter had worsened to one in five. The problem of long-term unemployment was also heavily concentrated among middle-aged and older people. In September 1929 one in every thousand insured men aged 18–24, four in every thousand aged 25–34, and fifteen in every thousand aged 55–64 had been unemployed for a year or more. In November 1932 the corresponding figures were twenty-five, thirty-two and seventy-four. By 1939 this contrast was even more marked with seven in every hundred men aged 55–64 victims of long-term unemployment compared with seven in every thousand men aged 18–24 (Phillipson 1977).

The problem of the older worker in relation to the new mass production industries had been noted by a study of social services in Oxford, published in 1938:

> The standard work in the motor industry is most suitable for fairly young men, and most of the employees are in fact young. It is feared that as they become elderly, they have some difficulty

keeping up with the demands of mass production; and if this is the case and they become unemployed, experience suggests that they will find it extremely difficult to find alternative employment.

(Survey Committee of Barnett House 1938)

For those unable to find work the social and financial pressures could be devastating. The *Birmingham Post* in December 1929 reported the following note left by an unemployed man who killed his wife and then committed suicide:

I feel so terribly worried, I am writing this while I am able to do so, for at times I go so strange I hardly know what to do with myself. My inside trembles, my head aches and I go dizzy, often on the verge of collapse, and even when crossing the road I fear I shall get knocked down. Sometimes I cross as in a dream. Therefore, if something happens it will not be the fault of the driver, but my own inability to get out of the way.

The note was signed, 'Frank Thornby, aged 62', with the postscript, 'Out of employment and can't get a job! The younger men get the jobs'.

The impact of the depression was to accelerate the shift away from employment after the age of 65; a change which appeared in the early part of the century, consolidated by the introduction of old age pensions, but which was undoubtedly hastened by the loss of jobs in the 1930s. Thus the economic activity rate for males over 65 moved from 65.4 per cent in 1891, to 56.8 per cent in 1911, down to 47.9 per cent in 1931. The period between 1931 and 1951 also showed a significant decline: among men 65–69 the rate fell from 65 to 49 per cent; for those 70–74 from 42 to 29 per cent; and for those 75 and over from 23 to 14 per cent. Working women also showed a similar tendency to leave the work-force in later life: the ratio of women over 65 still at work to the proportion of working women aged 25–64 fell from 65 per cent in 1881 to 43 per cent in 1911, and 16 per cent in 1951 (cited in Hannah 1986: 188).

The economic depression reinforced the stereotype of older workers as inefficient and unable to adapt to new technology. Achenbaum describes this period as having a 'devastating effect on the elderly [in America]', with high rates of unemployment coming alongside the bankruptcy of many pension plans (Achenbaum 1978: 128–9). Chudacoff (1989) notes that during the depression in America, Forty Plus Clubs were formed in many cities to help try to preserve jobs for older workers. However, he notes that 'during World War II most of these organizations dissolved. The over-forty groups complained that employers had no incentive to utilize their members, and that they were being discriminated against' (Chudacoff 1989: 173).

For a brief period in the later 1940s and 1950s, this image was to change, with the experience and reliability of older workers being highlighted in a context of labour shortages (Phillipson 1982; Harper and Thane 1989). However, this was to prove a relatively brief interlude. By the mid-1950s the need to retain older workers was substantially reduced. Indeed, by the 1960s and early 1970s numerous studies pointed to the employment difficulties of older workers in settings as diverse as mining (Department of Employment 1970) and car assembly (MacKay 1973). MacKay's work suggested that redundant car workers beyond their mid-forties stood a much lower chance than younger workers even of being re-engaged by their previous firm. Daniel's (1972) study of redundant workers at Woolwich indicated that the older the worker the greater the likelihood of lower earnings in any subsequent employment. Fogarty's (1975) comprehensive review, *40 to 60: How We Waste the Middle-Aged*, found a widespread tendency to bar middle-aged applicants from recruitment to professional and managerial jobs, a 'tendency [which] probably increased from the 1950s to the early 1970s' (Fogarty 1975: 83).

Older people and industrial re-organization

Older workers were, however, largely ignored in the context of what was seen as a more fundamental issue affecting British industry – the problem of overmanning. Low productivity came to be viewed as a major influence on Britain's poor (by international standards) economic performance, with government's searching for ways of rationalizing inefficient and unprofitable sectors of industry (Glyn and Sutcliffe 1972). Britain's own economic problems were deepened by the 'oil crisis' in the winter of 1973–4, a contributory factor in the international crash of 1974 (Armstrong *et al.* 1984). These elements combined to consolidate the rising levels of unemployment which had affected Britain by the late 1960s and early 1970s.

Against this background, the focus in staffing policy was on the need for redundancies, 'shake-outs' and early retirements. Britain's economic position (and the condition of her industry) demanded, it was argued, a smaller and more efficient work-force. Given also that the post-war baby boom was producing a surfeit of young workers, it was the replacement of the old with the young which emerged as a significant element in staffing policy (the Job Release Scheme, launched in 1977, is one example of this). Esping-Andersen (1990) suggests, in this context, that measures such as early retirement were invaluable to employers seeking to reduce their work-force. This was especially the case, he suggests, in those countries with strong trade unions and strict seniority rules within the work-place.

In Britain, one important means of influencing the age and occupational profile of industry was through the system of redundancy payments. These had been established by the Redundancy Payments Act 1965. The Act requires employers to make lump-sum payments to workers who lose their jobs because of reductions in the need for their labour. The thinking behind the legislation was that over-staffing was a major barrier to economic expansion and that payments would, first, secure greater acceptance of the need for technological change and, second, would help to redeploy workers to new jobs. In fact, the effects of the Act were felt most keenly by older workers, with age becoming an important criteria for determining those selected for redundancy (Parker 1971; Martin and Fryer 1973). A study by the Department of Employment concluded that '[redundancy acts] as a social mechanism [removing] from the labour force older people who are nearing retirement after long service, by means of comparatively generous compensation' (Jolly *et al.* 1980; see also House of Commons 1989: 96). And, of course, once having been made redundant, older workers (particularly those aged 60–64) tended either to remain unemployed or to enter early retirement.

In fact, given the pressures facing British industry from the late 1960s onwards, older workers were always likely to be the most directly affected. This is because in the period under discussion, Britain had an ageing work-force, particularly in industries such as agriculture, mining and vehicles (for men), and metal goods, textiles, food, gas, electricity and water (for women). The implications of this for the workers involved were spelt out in a study by the Department of Employment:

> In terms of the changing age profiles of industries it may be noted that the decline in older male employment is consistent with older men working in slow-growing industries with lower earnings, and that older females (whose employment has increased) are associated with undynamic labour-intensive industries. Neither in terms of the number employed nor of the work situation does the employment position of the older worker appear to be entirely satisfactory.
>
> (Jolly *et al.* 1980: 80)

The institutionalization of early exit

Older men and women's exit from the labour force was to accelerate throughout the 1970s and 1980s (Makeham 1980; Jackson 1984;

Walker 1984). Early retirement, as Laczko and Walker (1985) comment, emerged as the only policy measure to combat unemployment which was supported by both Left and Right of the political spectrum.

The growth of early retirement was, of course, closely linked to the emergence of mass unemployment. Indeed, as Jackson (1984) observes, its acceleration from the mid-1970s onwards must be seen 'as a response to unemployment rather than as the response to a demand for change on its own merits from any section of industry'. There were four key factors which consolidated the drift of older workers from employment:

1 The decline in semi-skilled and unskilled jobs (Bosanquet 1983)
2 The entry or re-entry into the labour market of women workers (see p.24), and the willingness of employers to accommodate them at lower wages (Townsend 1979)
3 The growth – through occupational pension schemes – of financial provision for early retirement on the grounds of ill-health (McGoldrick and Cooper 1989)
4 The growing number (albeit a minority) who chose early retirement as a positive and valued alternative to full-time work (McGoldrick and Cooper 1989).

Other causative factors exist, but they must be regarded as more speculative. For example there is some evidence that work disability is increasing at the same time as a decline in mortality rates (Feldman 1983; Verbrugge 1984). This may arise through improved survival rates for diseases which in the past were usually fatal. At present, however, disabled or partially disabled people are likely to be regarded by employers as suitable candidates for redundancy; alternatively they are the least likely to be selected for work by employers choosing from a large pool of unemployed people.

Despite the above points, the context of mass unemployment is crucial for understanding the dynamics of earlier retirement (Casey and Laczko 1989). Thus as many commentators have pointed out, present conditions may lead people to accept early retirement not because they really want to do so, but because of work-place pressure, or their own view that retirement may lead to a younger person getting a job. Such pressures may be felt most keenly by unskilled and semi-skilled workers, a group who are more likely than white-collar groups to suffer from ill-health and to work in industries experiencing long-term decline and/or technological change.

In conclusion, our arguments suggest that from the 1970s onwards, older workers were increasingly marginalized in the labour force. This arose through first, their concentration, in many cases, in contracting industries; second, the operation of particular schemes to promote worker redeployment (e.g. the Redundancy Payments Act) or replacement (the Job Release Scheme); third, the pressure of mass unemployment; fourth, changing attitudes among government, business, trade unions and older people themselves, in respect of the older workers right to employment in relation to other, younger age groups (Bytheway 1986; Walker 1989). In the next section, we analyse these processes in more detail, beginning with the dramatic changes in economic activity in the post-war period.

The decline of labour force participation

The economic activity rates of older workers have been falling throughout this century. Until the mid-1970s the decline was most marked among men over the age of 65. Since then there has been a considerable fall in the proportion of men aged 50–64 who are economically active. In 1951 just under one-third of men over the age of 65 were still economically active. In the decades that followed, this proportion fell and by 1986, only about one in fifteen of this age group were still in the labour market (Table 2.1). This was consistent with a generalization of the norm of retirement at the age of 65, and this can itself be seen as a product of increasing societal wealth, particularly in so far as this led to extension of eligibility for pensions – both public and private – and improvements in their value (Casey and Laczko 1989). At the same time, however, it should also be noted that since 1975 the labour force participation of men over retirement age has fallen almost twice as fast as during 1951–75.

More interesting is what has occurred to men under the age of 65. In 1951 nearly 90 per cent of men in the 60–64 age range were still in the labour market. This proportion fell only gradually until the mid-1970s. After 1975, however, the activity rate of 60–64-year-old men began to fall dramatically, and by 1986 it had come to stand at no more than 54 per cent. Equally, while about 95 per cent of all 55–59-year-old men were in the labour market in 1951, and about the same proportion in 1975, by 1986 the figure was only 80 per cent. In 1990 the participation rates of older people within five years of state retirement age were actually lower than for teenagers (Wells 1989).

The fall in participation rates occurred alongside a massive increase in unemployment, with those older workers who did become unemployed being the least likely to find new jobs. This suggests that there is likely to be a relationship between the overall level of unemployment and work-force participation among older people – a relationship confirmed in recent research (Casey and Laczko 1989).

Table 2.1 Labour force participation rates of older men, Britain 1951–88 (percentages)

Age		1951	1961	1966	1971	1975	1976	1979	1981	1983	1984	1985	1986	1988
55–59	(1)	95.0	97.1	95.4	95.3				91.5					
	(2)				93.0	93.0	92.4	90.8	89.4	84.1	82.1	82.0	80.3	
60–64	(1)	87.7	91.0	87.7	86.6				74.6					
	(2)				82.9	82.3	80.4	73.0	69.3	59.4	56.7	54.4	53.4	55.0
65+	(1)	31.1	25.0	23.5	19.2				10.7					
	(2)				19.3	15.6	14.5	10.3	10.3	8.1	8.2	8.2	7.4	8.0
Unemployment rate (men and women, all ages)														
	(3)	1.0	1.3	1.2	3.3				10.4					
	(4)				2.7	3.2	4.5	4.2	8.4	10.7	10.9	11.1	11.4	

Notes: 1 Census data
2 Department of employment estimates and *Labour Force Survey* data
3 Old series (registered unemployed)
4 New series (unemployed in receipt of benefits)

Sources: Employment Gazette (various issues); Census of Population for England and Wales and for Scotland (various years); Casey and Laczko 1989.

Table 2.2 Female economic activity rates, Britain 1951–83

	Age	1951	1961	1971	1973	1975	1980	1983
Married	45–54	23.7	35.3	57.0	63	67	67	68
females	55–59	15.6	26.0	45.5	48	49	52	52
	60–64	7.2	12.7	25.2	25	26	25	20
	65+	2.7	3.4	6.5	8	6	6	4
Non-married	45–54	67.2	75.5	78.1	74	77	74	67
females	55–59	50.9	63.1	67.2	69	62	64	53
	60–64	25.2	32.3	33.7	34	34	26	17
	65+	6.4	6.9	6.3	6	6	4	4

Sources: Social Trends 6, London 1975: 84; *Employment Gazette* December 1975; May 1987

This suggests that if unemployment had not risen as sharply as it did between 1975 and 1986, a further 400,000 men aged 55–64 would still have been economically active in 1986.

The experience of women

Women's economic activity rates can be seen to fluctuate over time according to their age and marital status (Tables 2.2 and 2.3). For women aged 55–59 the economic activity rates of women who were not married have been on a downward trend since 1971 (see Table 2.2). In 1973, for example, this age group had an economic activity rate of 69 per cent whereas in 1983 the percentage was 53 per cent. A similar trend is visible in the activity rates of married women between the ages of 60–64 and over 65 years old. For example married women aged 60–64 had an economic activity rate of 25 per cent in 1973 but only 20 per cent in 1983. Although the size of the rate varies, these trends are the same as those for men of the equivalent ages, that is 55–59, 60–64 and 65+. The fluctuations in the activity rates of these groups of older women and men are considerably greater than those visible in other age groups over the same periods. Married women aged 55–59 are the exception to these trends since they have economic activity rates which have increased during the 1970s and 1980s.

The British pattern of women's employment has some important differences in comparison to many European countries. Dale and Glover (1989) highlight a number of variations. First, countries with the lowest levels of female economic activity (Ireland, Luxembourg, Italy and Greece), where women's employment activity rates peak in

Table 2.3 Female economic activity rates, Britain 1971–91

Estimates

Age	1971	1972	1973	1974	1975	1976	1977	1978	1979	1980	1981	1982	1983	1984	1985	1986
45–54	60.6	63.2	64.8	66.0	66.3	66.5	66.7	66.9	67.0	67.6	66.0	68.1	68.1	69.2	69.4	70.2
55–59	51.1	51.1	51.4	51.9	52.4	54.3	56.1	55.0	53.8	53.6	53.4	52.0	50.6	51.1	51.8	51.7
60–64	28.2	28.8	28.7	28.7	28.6	26.9	25.2	23.3	21.5	22.4	23.3	21.9	20.5	21.3	18.6	18.8
65+	6.4	6.0	5.6	5.3	4.9	4.7	4.4	3.9	3.4	3.6	3.7	3.5	3.2	3.0	3.0	2.7

Projections

Age	1987	1988	1989	1990	1991
45–54	70.8	71.3	71.5	71.7	71.8
55–59	51.7	51.7	51.7	51.7	51.7
60–64	18.5	18.2	18.0	17.7	17.4
65+	2.7	2.6	2.5	2.5	2.4

Source: Employment Gazette May 1987

the early twenties and then follow a rapid decline right up until retirement age: in these countries, by the time women enter the 55–59 age group, we find participation rates have fallen to as low as around 20 per cent in the case of, for example, Italy and Ireland. Second, a group of countries with much higher rates of female employment (e.g. Britain, France and Denmark), these being maintained among the older age groups, where (in the British case) we find an activity rate which has fluctuated between 51 per cent and 55 per cent throughout the 1970s and 1980s (and is projected to continue at this level through the 1990s). The British pattern is somewhat distinctive when compared with other countries with high levels of female employment. Thus we have retained the pattern of a decline in employment from the mid-twenties through to the mid-thirties (as women leave work to raise a family), with a sharp increase in employment rates thereafter – approaching 70 per cent for women in their forties. In France, by comparison, women are more likely to stay in the labour force through their child-rearing years, with a gradual withdrawal from work as they enter their late forties.

Finally, any analysis of women's experience must also acknowledge age, period and generational influences affecting trends in employment. In the British case, these suggest, as we have noted, that the increase in women's participation in the labour force is particularly marked among women in their thirties and forties, and that this is largely in part-time rather than full-time work. Martin and Roberts (1984) confirmed this situation in their major survey of women's employment, a feature of which was its collection of detailed work histories covering female respondents' working lives since leaving full-time education. This study highlighted the increasing attachment to the labour force of women born later in the century, that is women of later birth cohorts. However, this factor is becoming less influential in raising activity rates. For those just below retirement age (55–59 years), it is almost certainly offset by moves to earlier retirement, these creating a convergence between the participation rates of older married and non-married women (the former remaining stable with the latter continuing their decline).

Taken overall, the declining level of participation of older women is probably a combined effect of, first, high unemployment in the 1970s and early 1980s; second, generational experiences (older women may belong to a generation less used to participating in paid work, particularly when married); third, health factors (either of the woman herself or of other members of the family); fourth, responsibilities in the area of informal care (the peak age for caring coming between the ages of 45 and 64).

Table 2.4 Estimates and projections of civilian activity rates (percentages)

	Age	1988	1995	2000
Men	55–59	80.4	81.8	81.8
	60–64	55.0	54.8	53.9
	65–69	12.3	8.6	6.7
	70+	5.4	4.1	3.4
	All ages	74.3	73.7	73.0
Women	55–59	52.8	53.6	53.6
	60–69	19.9	21.0	21.0
	70+	2.8	2.3	2.1
	All ages	51.1	53.6	54.5

Source: Department of Employment 1989b; quoted by Bosanquet *et al.* 1990

Table 2.5 Status of employed older men and women 1979, 1984 and 1988 (percentages)

	Aged 55–59			Aged 60–64			Aged 65–69		
	1979	1984	1988	1979	1984	1988	1979	1984	1988
Men									
Full-time employee	89	84	80	86	79	76	31	16	20
Part-time employee	1	2	2	3	5	6	48	44	44
Self-employed	9	14	18	10	16	17	19	39	35
All part time	3	4	6	5	8	11	53	65	62
Women									
Full-time employee	46	44	44	30	30	24	17	15	15
Part-time employee	48	48	47	61	63	63	71	66	64
Self-employed	5	7	8	8	11	13	10	18	22
All part time	50	54	51	65	73	72	77	75	79

Note: The first three rows sum to 100% and are based upon respondents' self-categorization. The fourth row defines as part-time all those (employees and self-employed) who usually work 30 or fewer hours per week.

Sources: Labour Force Surveys: Casey and Laczko 1991

Future trends

Official projections suggest that participation rates for men and women aged 60 are likely to fall still further up to the year 2000; those for men and women aged 55–59 will show very little change (Table 2.4). However, although overall employment levels for older workers may not increase markedly in the 1990s, this period is likely to be characterized by greater flexibility in work patterns (see also Chapter 3). This is because of a marked change in the labour market for older workers over the past ten years, with the increasing importance of self-employed people, part-time workers and female employees (Table 2.5). Across the British labour market as a whole there has been an increase in the proportion of people in 'non-standard' forms of employment (Hakim 1989). There has been a striking increase in self-employment, from 9 per cent of the total work-force in 1980 to 15 per cent in 1990. Among older workers the increase is even greater (see Table 2.5). A higher proportion of the labour force in self-employment implies that more people approaching retirement age will not face retirement at a fixed age. Traditionally, self-employed people are more likely to work beyond state pensionable age: first, because they can adjust their hours of work more easily; second, for financial reasons (they are unlikely to have index-linked pensions). A higher proportion of older workers in part-time work also suggests more flexibility, with more people likely to combine elements of work and retirement.

Conclusion: the political economy of retirement

The final task in this chapter is to place the above trends within the context of more general observations, first, about the institution of retirement; second, the treatment of older people in times of high unemployment. Historians and sociologists have now reached a rough consensus about some of the main reasons behind the development of retirement. These may be broadly summarized in terms of, first, the shift towards an advanced industrial economy and a specialized division of labour; second, improvements in living standards and the growth of more positive attitudes towards leisure; third, the development of private and state retirement schemes, with, in particular, the imposition of the retirement condition for receipt of the state pension.

In respect of the first point, a major influence was the growth of large-scale organizations and the bureaucratization of employment practices. Here Graebner (1980) makes the point that

> Retirement was one of several means available to a business-culture committed to restructuring the age component of the

workforce. Workers might be fired outright, of course, but . . .
such a policy was difficult for most public and private employers
to carry out. Retirement was impersonal and egalitarian in its
application. It allowed the powerful turn-of-the-century impulse
towards efficiency to co-exist with a system of labour relationships.

(Graebner 1980: 53)

Retirement, according to this line of argument, is bound-up with the
reconstitution of the labour force, within the context of the application of F. W. Taylor's theory of 'scientific management', the
'de-skilling' of the labour process and the break-up of the craft
hierarchy (Braverman 1974; Myles 1984; P. Thompson 1989). Of
additional importance was the shortening of the working day and the
associated speed up in production. One implication of this was, as
Graebner observes, that it was less the new technology which sealed
the fate of older workers, more the speed at which it was operated·

Employers apparently felt that the high capital costs of new
machinery could be justified only if that machinery were
operated at speeds that led inevitably to the obsolescence of older
workers too old to maintain required levels of productivity.

(Graebner 1989: 19; see also Morrison 1986)

In terms of the spread of retirement in the twentieth century, this has
also reflected the way in which older people have been sacrificed in
times of mass unemployment, with the priority being placed on jobs
for the young. In this regard, the expansion in the numbers entering
retirement (or becoming detached, on a permanent basis, from work)
must be seen as part of an attempted trade-off between one generation
and another (the reality being, as we shall argue in Chapter 6, that
relatively few jobs are created for the young by the enforced departure
of older people). But the pressures and insecurities placed upon older
workers is certainly one inevitable outcome. Alongside this has been a
hardening in the view, throughout this century, that a relationship
exists between age and declining capacities. Negative stereotypes
about the old developed during periods of rapid industrialization and
were consolidated in periods of economic recession (Phillipson 1982;
Morrison 1986). By the 1970s they had hardened into a set of
generalizations available for use as a means of justifying the premature
retirement of substantial numbers of workers. It is to the dynamics of
this process and to the nature of age discrimination that we now turn.

3

Ageing and discrimination in the labour market

Introduction

Chapter 2 described both the emergence of retirement and the trend towards early exit in the 1970s and 1980s. At the same time, we examined some of the pressures facing older workers in periods of economic recession and industrial reorganization in the labour market. This chapter will focus upon the question of age discrimination in more detail, relating this both to the historical context already outlined and research data on the abilities of older workers. The purpose of the chapter will be to answer a question of major importance as regards the work experience of older people: how do we explain the dramatic shift in activity rates (for older men especially) which occurred in the 1970s and 1980s? Does the answer lie solely in demand and supply factors operating within that particular time period? Alternatively or in addition, are there longer-run factors which need to be taken into account? Clearly answers to such questions are valuable both in terms of understanding the future employment prospects of older workers and as regards the ramifications for other areas of social policy (for example income maintenance and job creation).

The exclusion of older workers

On the basis of the historical research discussed in Chapter 2 it might be argued that well before the growth of early exit in the 1970s, a consensus had been reached that older workers were an expendable element in the labour force. By the late 1950s, notwithstanding the efforts of the Advisory Committee on the Employment of Older Men and Women (National Advisory Committee 1953; 1955), surveys were showing that first, the attentions of employers were focused almost exclusively around the problems faced by younger employees; second, as a consequence, few positive steps were taken to assist the retention of older workers in industry; third, there was clear evidence for the development of negative stereotypes about older workers (an important element in the phenomenon of ageism as it came to be defined by researchers such as Robert Butler in an article published in 1975). A survey in 1951 of the 400 member firms of the Industrial Welfare Society revealed that they had not attempted to consider, let alone assess, the profitability of employing older workers (Harper and Thane 1989). Another survey found that, even among the employers of skilled workers, one-third were doubtful as to the worth of those aged over 45 (Harper and Thane 1989).

The period of the 1950s was important, therefore, in confirming the policy established in the inter-war period, namely that older workers (and especially those over pensionable age) had both less need and less of a right to paid work. On the former, Rowntree (1947), in his report on older people, suggested that real poverty in old age had been virtually eliminated; a view which was to go virtually unchallenged until the publication in 1965 of Townsend and Wedderburn's *The Aged in the Welfare State*. On the latter, there was a hardening of the view – among both trade unions and employers – that older workers should, through more generous state and occupational pensions, be allowed to leave the labour force (Hannah 1986). For both groups this was seen as a mechanism for expanding the routes to more senior jobs and for increasing the supply of jobs to younger workers. It also reflected a growing belief on the part of employers that older workers were simply less efficient and less productive.

This post-war consensus was to provide the underpinning for the acceleration of early exit in the 1970s. This can be seen in two senses: first, the idea of retirement began to be established in a more substantial form in this period (Atchley 1988). True, the overwhelming image was a negative one (at least in the UK), with the prevailing view of retirement being that of a short period of boredom followed by premature death (Phillipson 1982). But steps were taken to promote a more positive view (for example, the rise of the pre-retirement movement in the USA and Britain in the 1950s and 1960s, Phillipson 1981). In addition, we see very little active resistance to the experience of exclusion from work once a certain age had been reached. In the 1950s and 1960s that point hovered around 60 for women and 65 for men; but clearly there was nothing fixed about these ages. Having confirmed the limited opportunities for work after pensionable age, the stage was set for further moves towards age discrimination at increasingly younger ages.

Occupational downgrading and age limits

The exclusion of older workers can be assessed in at least two ways: first, as measured by unemployment rates; second, in respect of age discrimination and occupational downgrading. In general terms, the unemployment rate of older workers in advanced industrialized countries tends to be below that of younger workers (OECD 1988b). However, once unemployed older workers are much more likely to experience long-term unemployment than younger workers (Spence 1990). Before the major world recession which began in the mid-1970s, long-term unemployment mainly affected older workers. For example in 1970, when unemployment in Britain stood at 2.6 per cent, over half of the long-term unemployed (people out of work for more than twelve months) were over the age of 55. As unemployment rose from the 1970s onwards, the composition of the long-term unemployed changed and an increasing share of the long-term unemployed has been taken by young workers and adults with families. In 1989, 80 per cent of the long-term unemployed were under the age of 55. None the less, older workers should they become unemployed, still have the highest risk of experiencing long-term unemployment, and in particular very long-term unemployment. In 1989, 7 per cent of unemployed 16–24-year-olds said they had been without a job and seeking work for three years or more, compared with 19 per cent of those aged 25–44 and 44 per cent of those between 45 and retirement age. These figures are all the more remarkable when it is remembered that the proportion of older workers in the labour force declined sharply throughout the 1980s.

Moreover, as was observed by many researchers in the 1930s (Pilgrim Trust 1938), when unemployment begins to fall older workers are among the last to be re-employed. The fall in unemployment which occurred in the mid-80s had most impact on shorter-duration unemployment amongst all age groups and on long-duration unemployment in younger age groups. It has had much less impact on long-duration unemployment among those over 45. The number of people over 45 unemployed for more than five years even rose slightly in the late 1980s. At this point there were still over a quarter of a million people aged over 45 who had been officially unemployed for more than two years (Bosanquet 1987). At the same time, the situation of older workers was to deteriorate further as unemployment rose again in the early 1990s.

Many more older workers who are effectively unemployed do not feature in the official figures because they have become discouraged from looking for work (see Table 3.1). Not all people who would like work and are available for work are classified as unemployed. Some

Table 3.1 Demographic composition of discouraged workers
(percentages)

	Total (thousands = 100 per cent)	Age			
		16–24	25–49	50–59	60–64 (males)
All					
1984	194	10.3	37.1	33.0	35.4
1987	132	7.5	33.3	37.1	33.7
Males					
1984	109	9.2	28.4	26.6	35.4
1987	83	*	31.3	27.5	33.7
Females					
1984	85	11.8	48.2	42.1	—
1987	49	*	37.8	53.7	

Note: * Less than 10,000 in cell, estimate not shown.

Sources: Labour Force Surveys 1984; 1987; Wells 1989

are classified in the UK Labour Force Survey (LFS) as economically inactive when they are not looking for work because they do not think any jobs are available (for a discussion of the definition of a 'discouraged worker' used in the Labour Force Survey, see Laczko 1987). The discouraged worker effect is most pronounced among older workers and is associated with their greater vulnerability to long-term unemployment (Laczko 1987; Wells 1989). Discouragement among older workers rose sharply after 1979 (Casey and Laczko 1989) and since 1984 has declined only marginally, whereas among younger workers there has been a considerable fall in the number of discouraged workers (Wells 1989).

Discrimination in the work-place

Apart from unemployment, occupational downgrading and age discrimination has also been the fate of many older workers. Thus, it is well established that men who experience a period of unemployment after 55 tend to move into lower-grade and lower-paid jobs (Daniel 1974; Daniel and Stilgoe 1977). Moreover, the existence of age limits for vacancies prevents older workers from being able to apply for many jobs. This is particularly evident for workers in the professional and managerial sector. In an analysis of Professional and Executive Recruitment (PER) vacancies in the 1970s, it was found that vacancies were invariably restricted to people below the age of 45 and above the age of 20 (Berthoud 1979). Only 11 per cent of PER vacancies were open to candidates over the age of 55. Age limits are often justified by management on the grounds that there is a need to maintain a progressive career structure within enterprises (Jolly *et al.* 1980). In the most comprehensive study of the use of age limits in employment, Jolly, Creigh and Mingay (1980) analysed age limits in jobs notified to the public employment service. This research showed that 27.5 per cent of public employment service vacancies notified to the Employment Services Division had upper age limits. Further evidence on age limits came in a survey by the Equal Opportunities Commission (1989). They monitored 11,373 job advertisements across a range of periodicals. Over 25 per cent of the advertisements stated an age preference. Almost all mentioned the age of 45 or under; 65 per cent of the adverts mentioning age gave a limit of 35 or under.

Age limits also tend to differ between occupational groups. The survey of Jolly and colleagues found that unskilled manual vacancies were the least likely to have upper age limits (18.5 per cent) and those vacancies which were age limited had the lowest proportion limited to those aged under 55 (87 per cent). Moreover, age limits were more rigidly enforced in non-manual occupations. Jolly *et al.* (1980) also examined the use of age limits in connection with entry to various occupations. The main finding was that the more an occupation is regarded as a career, the more likely it is to limit entry to particular age groups. This explains in part why older workers who become unemployed tend to move into lower-paid, lower-grade work, should they find employment, as age limits tend to be less important in these jobs.

The existence of age discriminatory recruitment practices is further illustrated by studies of the experience of professional employees. In a study of unemployed professionals and executives carried out in 1977, Berthoud found little evidence to suggest that the higher level of long-term unemployment among older professionals and executives could be explained by a weaker desire to find work or by differences in their characteristics as compared with younger job-seekers. Berthoud suggests that the problem does not lie with the individual:

> We found no explanation, within the data available to us, why the middle-aged should do so poorly in the search for new jobs. It is not because they suffer from ill-health, not because they lack academic qualifications, not because they do not make a serious

attempt, not because having been made redundant from one particular job, they might be considered redundant in a wider sense.

(Berthoud 1979: 83)

Instead, the problem lies partly in the highly developed career structure and the internal labour market from which most professionals and executives derive so much benefit (see p. 38). At the same time, it also stems from the attitudes of people responsible for hiring older workers. Ageism is still an alien word in the UK (unlike the USA), and there have been very few academic studies of age discrimination (however, see Slater 1973; Slater and Kingsley 1976). In part this may be because

> Nothing in age, not any particular age, corresponds to the relatively clear-cut distinctions of race and sex; so age discrimination is less palpable and goes unrecognised. People are quite ready to accept as final a statement that they are too old for the job, even when this is untrue, in a way that they would no longer accept that they are the wrong colour/sex.
>
> (Baboulene 1976)

Sinfield has also drawn attention to the ageism which is reflected in the acceptance of greater long-term unemployment among older workers.

> Demands for government action to reduce unemployment are frequently supported by . . . 'It's even hitting the family man now – not just the old'. The observer would note that in Britain it is more acceptable for the old or unskilled to be unemployed – our sense of what is proper and normal is less offended.
>
> (Sinfield 1976: 223; see also McEwan 1990)

There have been some studies of employers' attitudes towards older workers. A Gallup (1990) survey on ageism in employment found 86 per cent of the employers surveyed regarded workers under age 35 as being most appropriate to their needs; almost as many said that they could not foresee a time when they would have to employ anyone over the official retirement age. In age discrimination women fare much worse than men: 36 per cent of employers said that a woman with the same skills and same age as a man would be more likely to be turned down because of her age. A number of studies of unemployed people have confirmed that older workers themselves believe that their age is a major handicap when applying for jobs. Many older unemployed people give up looking for work because they consider that they have little chance of finding work. In one study of the long-term unemployed it was found that 40 per cent of those aged 55–59 and 60 per cent of those aged 60–64 thought they had 'no chance' of finding another job (Colledge and Bartholomew 1980). In another major survey of the long-term unemployed it was noted that 'older workers quite explicitly blamed age discrimination on the part of employers for their failure to obtain work' (White 1983: 58).

Discrimination against older workers is not only evident among employers, but also exists within the public employment service, which is responsible for providing individuals with information about vacancies. The government employment services tend to allocate their assistance primarily towards younger workers and people unemployed for a short duration. Job creation and training schemes have tended to focus almost exclusively on younger people. Employers' discrimination against older workers, therefore, tends to be reflected and reinforced by the public employment service's failure to refer older people for jobs (see p. 35).

Training and education

Older workers also tend to be at a disadvantage when applying for jobs in today's labour market simply because they belong to a generation which has had fewer years of schooling. Older workers are at a relative disadvantage because individuals without any formal qualifications are more likely to experience unemployment (Wells 1989). The majority of older workers in a study of redundancy and early retirement from the steel industry had received minimal education and little training (Walker *et al*. 1985: 328). This lack of formal education and training may not be a problem within an organization but is likely to become a particular handicap when older workers have to compete for jobs in the external labour market. Changes in the occupational structure of the work-force over time, and in particular the decline in unskilled and semi-skilled jobs, makes it more difficult for older workers with few skills to find employment. Each succeeding generation of young workers tends to have jobs of higher occupational status than their predecessors (Townsend 1979: 667).

The lack of education and training of older workers is exacerbated by the limited interest shown in retraining older people. By far the highest amount of training goes to 16–19-year-olds, with 23 per cent getting some form of training in the four weeks before the 1989 LFS, compared to just 7 per cent for 50–64-year-olds (Spence 1990). These figures stayed virtually the same throughout the 1980s, despite warnings to employers about the need to retrain older workers. Failure to retrain appears to be a problem facing older employees at all levels. Thus a study by Coulson-Thomas (1990), entitled *Too Old at*

40, highlighted the lack of initiatives, education and training programmes available for older managers. Many faced being pushed into
early retirement schemes to let younger people have a better chance of
advancement within the organization.

Employers are often not prepared to retrain older workers because
they believe it is too expensive to employ older workers given that they
will remain in employment for a shorter period than younger workers
(Ashton 1986). Moreover, there is a belief on the part of some
employers that older workers are less adaptable and not prepared to
retrain (International Labour Organization 1979: 29). Neither does
government help in setting an example in the area of training. The
Employment Training scheme designed to assist the long-term
unemployed, concentrates almost exclusively on under-50-year-olds;
over-60-year-olds are not eligible to participate. Only 5 per cent of
people receiving 'Employment Training' are over the age of 50 (House
of Commons 1989: 105). Finally, it should be noted that despite
expressions of concern about an ageing work-force, the Department
of Employment has never carried out a specific study of the training
needs of the over-fifties.

Ageing and performance in employment

Age discrimination may, of course, be justified on a number of
grounds by an employer. In particular, he or she may view such a
policy as essential given the need for a labour force which can adapt
quickly to changes in technology and manpower requirements within
the firm or organization. In this context, even analysts sympathetic to
the unemployed see older workers as a problem. Ashton (1986: 80),
for example, cites two main difficulties with an ageing work-force:
'first and foremost . . . because of the tendency for workers'
productive capacity to decline with age; second, because they are less
able to adapt to the new requirements posed by technological change'.
Yet what is striking to observe here is that forty years of research in the
field of industrial gerontology provides no support for such views.
Doering and his colleagues (1983) have provided the most exhaustive
review of research in this area. They made a detailed analysis of
twenty-eight empirical studies of the age–performance relationship.
Their conclusions were that the performance of older workers is not
necessarily either better or worse than that of younger workers but
that other factors such as level of motivation, self-reliance, recognition, experience, and job demands may influence performance with
age.

These points were also brought out in the review by Parker (1982) where he noted that productivity was affected only minimally if at all by age. He went on to suggest that changes brought about by ageing have been alleged to reduce employability in several different ways: first, physical (e.g. loss of strength); second, temperamental (e.g. increased emotionality); third, cognitive (e.g. difficulty with short-term memory) and, finally, personality (e.g. loss of confidence). However, Parker goes on to make the important point that

> The short answer to these claims is that some elderly workers do show some of these changes some of the time, but it is relatively rare for a particular individual to show all such changes. Some people are very effective in compensating for particular handicaps or shortcomings and [they may also have] other qualities and attributes which younger people do not have, or have to a less degree.
>
> (Parker 1982: 86)

The research on which these arguments are based tends, however, to be put aside at times when it is politically and economically expedient. This was certainly the case in the late 1950s when the Advisory Committee on the Employment of Older Men and Women was terminated (National Advisory Committee 1953; 1955). The Chairman recalled that wide publicity had been given to the committee's two reports and there was evidence of 'considerable success in breaking down the traditional barriers against the employment of older workers' (Ministry of Labour 1959: 26). It was also emphasized that the winding-up of the committee did not mean that 'the government had lost interest in the employment of older workers' (Ministry of Labour 1959: 27). However, when at the beginning of 1959 the Minister of Labour was asked how many men had been forced into retirement as a consequence of the trade depression over the previous twelve months, the reply came: 'I regret that statistics giving the information are not available' (*Hansard* vol. 599: col. 59). Harper and Thane summarized the position:

> By the beginning of the 1960s, the government had given up the attempt to encourage employers to take special note of the needs of older workers. In 1964, the annual Labour Gazette stopped printing annual retirement figures. Fears of a national labour shortage had eased and were replaced by fears of large-scale unemployment due to the spread of 'automation'. . . . The abolition of national service, Commonwealth immigration, the entry into the labour market of the 'baby boom' generation, and the increasing numbers of married women remaining in or returning to work all provided additional supplies of labour. To

what extent they provided substitutable labour for older, skilled
workers is another, unresearched, question; but, in general,
interest in older workers as a source of labour and in the effects of
their work and retirement status on their own health and that of
the national economy waned.

(Harper and Thane 1989: 57; see also Welford 1976)

This last point was equally the case in the 1970s and early 1980s as
governments stressed the virtues of retirement in an age of mass
unemployment; stressing, at the same time, the problems faced by
older workers given the pace of technological change.

Labour market theory and the older worker

So far we have documented both the extent of older people's exclusion
from work and the degree of age discrimination within the labour
market. In this section we examine a number of approaches and
theories that have been used to understand these developments and
assess how they relate to the emergence of retirement. Let us
consider, first of all, theories which attempt to explain the problems
faced by older people in the work-place. A number of criticisms have
emerged of approaches taken by classical economists to explaining
disadvantages and inequalities in the labour market. These perspectives challenge the view that all vacancies in the economy are
continually open to all workers on the same terms and conditions, and
suggest instead that the labour market is divided into a number of
segments. The classical view holds that workers with similar training
and ability should receive the same earnings and that the price of
labour is determined by 'pure' market forces (Townsend 1979: 645).
The theories of labour market segmentation, in contrast, link together
pay differentials with occupational segregation, poverty, and race and
sex discrimination (Dex 1989). However, these theories make little
mention of age discrimination, or the specific problems of older
workers. The best-known model of labour market segmentation is
that put forward by Piore (1975), which is known as 'dual labour
market theory' (see also Hendricks and McAllister 1983). This model
suggests that the labour market is divided into two distinctive
segments. The main elements of the model are as follows:

The basic hypothesis of the dual labour market [is] that the
labour market is divided into two essentially distinct sectors,
termed primary and secondary sectors. The former offers jobs
with relatively high wages, good working conditions, chances of
advancement, equity . . . and above all, employment security.

Jobs in the secondary sector, by contrast, tend to be low paying with poor working conditions, little chance of advancement, a highly personalized relationship between workers and supervisors which leads to wide latitude for favouritism and is conducive to hard and capricious work discipline and with considerable instability in jobs and high turnover among the labour force.

(Piore 1975: 126; quoted by Dex 1989)

The segmentation of the labour market is said to be caused by a number of factors such as discrimination, either on the basis of sex or ethnic background, low education, and institutional restrictions. Since the theory of the dual labour market was first conceived it has been subject to a substantial amount of criticism. The key points may be summarized: first, the theory provides no operational definition of 'good' and 'bad' jobs; second, mobility between the primary and secondary sector exists and the wage structure shows no evidence of bipolarization (Addison and Siebert 1979); third, the models of labour market careers posited by the theory tend to be oversimplifications – for instance some low-paid jobs are stable and have relatively low turnover rates; finally, the dual labour market model also tends to be somewhat 'static' and does not explain how labour market position changes according to age or according to alterations in the structure of the work-force over time.

None the less, the dual labour market model does provide a useful framework for understanding the labour market experience of many older workers. First, discussion of segmented labour markets resulted in the introduction of the concept of an 'internal labour market' which was suggested to be a feature of the primary sector (Doeringer and Piore 1971). Internal labour markets are those in which the competition for jobs is restricted to internal candidates within the organization. The internal labour market is

an administrative unit such as a manufacturing plant within which the pricing and allocation of labour is governed by a set of administrative rules and procedures in contrast with the external labour market where decisions are controlled directly by economic variables. Movements between the two markets occur at certain job classifications which constitute ports of entry and exit to and from the internal labour market. The remainder of jobs within the internal labour market are filled by the promotion or transfer of workers who have already gained entry.

(Doeringer and Piore 1971; quoted by Makeham 1980: 42)

The existence of internal labour markets helps to explain why older workers are less likely on the one hand to become unemployed, but more likely to experience long-term unemployment if they do become unemployed. It has been suggested that a major distinction must be made between the attitudes of firms to older workers already in their employment and to older workers seeking employment (Makeham 1980: 25). Older workers in the internal labour market benefit from practices such as pay scaled by age and other seniority provisions. In the internal labour market, favourable treatment is given to existing as opposed to potential employees by means of promotion ladders internal to the firm and ports of entry limited to low levels of skill. Employers according to the segmented labour market approach recruit predominantly at the lowest grades, the higher grades being filled internally, often on the basis of seniority (Adnett 1989). This makes it difficult for older workers who are not in employment to become re-employed. Older workers who are seeking employment will tend to be limited to vacancies with a low skill-level content and therefore may be confined to a secondary labour market (Makeham 1980). These points have been summarized by Shrank and Waring (1989) in their exploration of what they see as 'organizational ambivalence' towards older workers. They point out that organizations tend to accord older employees higher earnings, greater power and better jobs. Yet they also note that

> being an older worker in many organizations also means being more vulnerable and insecure . . . being encouraged to take early retirement, or simply set aside or even terminated, often to be replaced by younger, generally lower-paid workers. Organizations send out contradictory signals to the older worker, they develop mixed and inconsistent policies, and encourage ambivalent social policies.
>
> (Shrank and Waring 1989: 115)

Older people as a reserve army of labour

In terms of demand-side factors, an attempt to explain what happens to older workers has come from those adopting the Marxist concept of the reserve army of labour. This idea refers to the tendency of capitalist economies to generate surplus working populations. According to Shirley Dex,

> When total capital is increasing, the demand for labour is expected to fall. Some workers will become redundant in the industry of their current employment, and workers will also be engaged at lower rates than previously. This 'freed' population is then available to be absorbed into new industries. There is also a

cyclical function for the reserve since the alternate periods of higher production and stagnation both effect and rely upon the reserve's formation.

(Dex 1985: 194)

In the case of older people, it might be argued that the idea of the reserve army of labour has somewhat limited utility, given the historical decline in the labour participation of older men independent of cyclical fluctuations in the economy (Johnson 1989a). However, three points might be made in support of the thesis: first, as has been argued in Chapter 2, older workers appear to be subject to high rates of displacement (or early exit) in times of recession. Second, we should note the ideological as well as economic function of the notion of a labour reserve. Here, the idea of a group (such as elderly people) being permanently 'on call' either to be re-employed or expelled from the labour force, may be valuable both in terms of the regulation and control of labour and as regards the allocation of benefits to older and retired workers; these being reduced on the grounds that part-time work/self-employment may be available. Third, the thesis draws our attention – at both macroeconomic and microeconomic levels – to the selective way in which the labour market may be manipulated. In general terms, in the 1970s and 1980s, we can see policies encouraging either early or deferred retirement in situations of both labour surpluses (in the 1970s and early 1980s) and labour shortages (in certain geographical areas and industries from the late 1980s and early 1990s onwards). A central mechanism underpinning the role of older people as a labour reserve has been mandatory retirement. Parker (1980), for example, found that approximately half of male respondents and one-fifth of female respondents were compulsorily retired at pension age. Dale and Bamford (1988) note that other research indicates that where there is flexibility as regards retirement age this is most frequently offered in the form of early retirement, and only rarely as deferred retirement.

Such policies appeared geared to the employers' desire to reduce 'head count' rather than to provide employees with a choice over the timing of their withdrawal from the labour force. Thus early retirement may be used as a mass form of redundancy, achieving job reduction in a socially acceptable way but at the expense of older workers.

(Dale and Bamford 1988: 45; see also Institute of Manpower Studies 1983; 1987)

It might also be suggested that in terms of the last decade the operation of a labour reserve in respect of older workers has operated in two distinctive ways. In the case of men, we find the maintenance of either lifetime employment or early retirement/unemployment up to state retirement age; thereafter, a substantial increase in the proportion defined as working part-time or self-employed. As regards women, the position is reversed, with a higher proportion of women than men engaged in full-time work after state pension age, though with a majority still working part-time. This erosion of gender differences in employment is also reflected in the industrial distribution of workers after pensionable age, with a clustering of older people in industries which use a high proportion of part-time workers. Dale and Bamford (1988) suggest in their analysis 'that age and statutory retirement policies are great levellers and that beyond retirement age those peripheral forms of work which characterise women's employment become dominant for men also'. They conclude that

it may be that the continued growth of the service sector and the associated availability of part-time jobs will allow at least some older workers to retain a toe hold in the labour market – albeit in jobs which are poorly paid and low status. In these circumstances, it would appear that women may be better able than men to retain employment into old age and that part-time service sector jobs taken in earlier years may prove an important source of employment beyond state retirement age.

(Dale and Bamford 1988: 60)

More generally, it might be argued that the experience of older people reflects the position of different groups within the welfare state, as outlined in an analysis by Claus Offe (1984):

The reliable and permanent incorporation of 'additional' labour power into the wage-labour market can be guaranteed only by strictly regulating the conditions under which non-participation in the labour market is possible (and where purely repressive measures like the punishment of begging and theft do not suffice). The choice between a life of wage labour and forms of subsistence outside the labour market must accordingly not be left to the discretion of labour power. When, and for how long, individuals remain outside the labour market, the decision whether someone is too old, sick, young, disabled, or has a valid claim to be part of the education system or to social provision must be left neither to individual needs nor to the momentary chances of subsistence outside the market. These choices must be positively regulated through politically defined criteria, for otherwise there would be incalculable tendencies for wage-labourers to evade their function by slipping into the flanking sub-systems. This is why a pre-condition of the constitution of a class of wage labourers is the political institutionalisation – and not merely the *de facto* maintenance – of various categories of non-wage-labourers.

(Offe 1984: 95)

Offe's point explains *inter alia* why the idea of a truly flexible retirement (with people going early or late according to their choice) is in practice so difficult to achieve. It presupposes a degree of freedom for wage labourers which is in sharp contradiction to many other aspects of their lives. The extent of tension between reforms in the field of retirement and areas relating to work is an issue we shall return to in Chapter 7.

The break-up of the life course

A final way of explaining the changes affecting older workers can be seen in terms of what both Martin Kohli and Anne-Marie Guillemard have described as the 'de-standardization of the life course' (Kohli 1986; Guillemard 1989). The argument here is that the development of early exit represents the break-up of the type of retirement which was established in the 1950s and 1960s. Thus it has been argued that in this period retirement at 60 or 65 became widely established (Parker 1982). Indeed, 'By the late 1960s it was accepted that the normal period of full-time economic employment would cease for most of the population at these ages' (Thane and Harper 1989: 59). However, it could be argued that this consolidation was a temporary phenomenon, merely a staging post to a much more fundamental change to the organization of the life course. On the one side, retirement did indeed emerge as a distinct phase in the life course (Phillipson 1978); but its starting-point and the range of statuses and roles within it were to become much more fluid from the late 1970s onwards (Laczko 1989). The transition into retirement is now being organized on a much more flexible basis (the notion of a decade of retirement between 60 and 70 being one manifestation of this), with a range of different pathways which people take before they either describe themselves or are defined within the social security system as 'wholly retired'. As a consequence of this, Guillemard argues that

The retirement system has lost its central function of regulating labour force withdrawal. The other subsystems (principally unemployment compensation and disability insurance) that now do this introduce their own logic for regulating the transition from work to non-work. As a result of this replacement of retirement, the chronological milestones that used to mark the life course are no longer visible; and functional criteria have assumed importance in organising the later years of life. . . . The time for definitive withdrawal for the individual is no longer fixed ahead of time; it is not predictable. Since the chronological milestones of retirement are being torn up, the threefold model, which placed the individual in a foreseeable lifecourse of continuous, consecutive sequences of functions and statuses, is coming apart.

(Guillemard 1989: 176–7)

In consequence, Guillemard argues, we are seeing increasing un- certainty as regards the position of older workers – both in their attitudes towards leaving work and in their position within the social and class structure.

Retirement and the modernization of ageing

Yet we might want to raise a number of critical comments in relation to the argument advanced by Guillemard. Does the idea of the 'break-up' of the life course adequately convey what is happening to the institution of retirement and to the experience of retired people in the 1990s? What are the causes of the changes which are taking place? What are the likely outcomes that can be identified? In this final section of the chapter we review some of the answers that might be made to these questions and consider, as well, some theoretical questions to be explored in later sections of this book.

The first issue we have to tackle is how we relate patterns of early exit to the wider changes affecting the economy in the post war period. One approach is suggested by David Harvey (1989) in his important study, *The Condition of Post Modernity*. Harvey notes that the post-war period saw the rise of a series of industries based on technologies which had matured in the inter-war years. At the same time, the state took on a number of new roles within the context of Keynesian demand management. This mixture of political and industrial strategies he terms as Fordist-Keynesian, which he defines as a network of arrangements built upon a certain set of labour control practices, technological mixes, consumption habits, and configur- ations of economic and political power. These factors formed an important backdrop to the history of retirement in the post-war period. They created the basis for long-term job security (for men though not for women), out of which the idea of retirement achieved some degree of social acceptability (again, the gender difference here is crucial) as part of the contract for an extended period of work. They also helped to consolidate a range of occupational benefits which could be used to underpin state benefits in retirement (again, either denied to or made available at lower levels to women). However, the argument raised by Harvey is that the 'Fordist compromise', as it may be termed, which underpinned these benefits, has been weakened by the economic recession which affected capitalist economies from the early 1970s onwards. Harvey observes that the

> 1970s and 1980s have subsequently been troubled period of economic restructuring and social and political readjustment. In the social space created by all this flux and uncertainty, a series of novel experiments in the realm of industrial organisation have begun to take shape. These experiments may represent the early stirrings of the passage to an entirely new regime of accumulation, coupled with quite a different system of political and social regulation.
>
> (Harvey 1989: 145)

Harvey uses the term 'flexible accumulation' to describe what he sees as some of the essential features of the new economic environment. The key point of note is that he sees it as an attempt to break from the rigidities of Fordism, particularly in terms of creating greater flexibility in respect of labour markets, labour processes, products and patterns of consumption. Given this analysis, we need to place the development of early exit within the context of moves towards more flexible work regimes and labour contracts. Indeed, we might explore the extent to which early exit itself is bound-up with this restructuring within the labour force.

To assess the above argument it is useful to distinguish at least two phases in the recent history of retirement. The first phase, as identified above, was the consolidation of retirement between 1950 and 1970 (Phillipson 1978; Harper and Thane 1989). This period was marked by fairly rigid age grading within industry (a process which was the culmination of a process which started in the mid-nineteenth century), the growth of occupational pension entitlements (Hannah 1986), and the gradual acceptance of retirement as a fixed and predictable point in the life course (Phillipson 1990a). Sociologically we can also identify this period as one in which retirement is viewed as a largely male phenomenon (and problem), one which reflected tensions in the movement from work to leisure (Parker 1982).

The second phase of retirement, from the 1970s onwards, is marked by a number of critical changes, these brought about by the move towards the more flexible work regimes described above. These changes may have influenced less a 'break-up', more a reconstruction of both middle and old age. Featherstone and Hepworth (1989) describe this in terms of the 'modernization of ageing', a development involving a 'distancing from deep old age – a distancing which is achieved through flexible adjustments to the gradually blurring boundaries of adult life' (Featherstone and Hepworth 1989: 154). This flexibility itself impacts on the transition to retirement (in ways we shall analyse in some detail in Chapter 4), with the growth, as we have suggested, of different work categories and statuses in between full-time work and complete retirement. Alongside this there is the move away from the expectation of lifetime employment within a single organization; the convergence of male and female employment trends (with what has been termed the 'feminization' of employment: Schuller 1989); and the growth of leisure as an important feature of daily life (Deem 1986; Glyptis 1989; Long 1989). The implications of these changes for an institution such as retirement is as yet unclear, however, some speculations will form the basis of Chapter 9. What is certain is that in the 1990s we have reached a new phase in the history of retirement. It is to the characteristics of this phase that we now turn.

4

Social policy and early exit

Introduction

The aim of this chapter is to examine in more detail the new phase of retirement, which developed from the 1970s onwards. We shall explore some of the key changes which took place in the 1970s and 1980s, focusing in particular on the various routes taken by older workers when moving out of the labour market. This chapter will seek to show that although more older workers may be considered to be retired in terms of the accepted meaning of 'giving up work' (Parker 1982), many older people who may be labelled as retired neither receive a retirement pension nor see themselves as retired. The implications of this for changes in the meaning and significance of retirement will also be examined. First, however, before outlining the pattern of early exit that has developed in recent years and the policies that have facilitated this process, it may be useful to remind ourselves of the objectives of early retirement schemes and how these have changed in recent years.

Early retirement and employment policy

The stated objectives of all early retirement programmes can be grouped under two main headings: 'social goals' and 'labour market goals'. Early retirement has long been a social policy objective of trade unions in Britain, as in other countries. Trade unions have argued that early retirement has a number of advantages for the individual, not least for manual workers who, on average, live to spend fewer years in retirement and who are more likely to suffer ill-health in later life as a result of working many years in arduous employment. A fixed retirement age is deemed to discriminate unfairly against manual workers who join the work-force at an early age, contribute for a longer period of years, yet survive to enjoy their pension for a shorter period of retirement than the average person (Whitehead 1989).

Early retirement measures are therefore intended to ease the workload and promote the health of older workers with long-standing illnesses, as well as equalize retirement opportunities between manual workers and non-manual workers. An additional objective is to give individuals greater flexibility so that they can choose when to retire, according to their needs and wishes.

However, demands for a lower retirement age based on social grounds found relatively little favour among governments and employers until unemployment began to rise in the mid-1970s. Since then, early retirement has been used increasingly as an instrument for realizing labour market objectives. For both unions and management, early retirement is regarded as a relatively uncontroversial means of reducing the work-force. It enables companies to avoid compulsory redundancies and is a more socially acceptable means of reducing labour (Institute of Manpower Studies 1983). Trade unions, in particular, tend to be in favour of early retirement because it reduces the likelihood of dismissals among younger workers who are usually entitled to lower redundancy payments because these are based on seniority and age. The use of early retirement schemes to persuade their least productive workers to give up work may also provide management with an easier method for controlling the shape of the work-force than other measures such as natural wastage or the last-in-first-out principle (Institute of Manpower Studies 1983).

Early exit options

Given the above context, what are the types of routes out of the labour market which have developed or have been used during the 1970s and 1980s? There are four key routes to identify in terms of early exit or early retirement:

1 the occupational pension route
2 public pre-retirement (the job release scheme)
3 the unemployment route
4 the disability route.

We shall now examine the characteristics of each of these routes or pathways, exploring issues relating to gender and class inequalities in terms of access and outcomes as the discussion proceeds.

The occupational pension route

To a large extent it has been left to employers in Britain to make provision for early retirement. One effect of this has been to extend occupational inequalities into the retirement period. Employers are able, and can afford to offer early retirement, only where employees are entitled to an occupational pension and have accrued significant pension rights under the terms of such a scheme. Employers have less scope to use early retirement to reduce the number of older manual workers and female workers in their work-force as these workers are less likely to have an occupational pension or if they do have such a pension it is more likely to be too low to finance early retirement (Institute of Manpower Studies 1983). A survey by the Equal Opportunities Commission in 1983 found only 52 per cent of male manual workers and 18 per cent of female manual workers to be members of occupational pension schemes; in the case of non-manual workers the figures were 72 per cent for men and 40 per cent for women. Male non-manual workers working in the public sector also have greater opportunities to retire early because jobs in this sector tend to have a lower retirement age. Examples of employers providing retirement before 65, include the civil service (60), British Rail (62), teachers (60), BBC (60), National Health Service (60) and the Post Office (60). Local government employees with twenty-five years' service can retire at any age between 60 and 65. In the public and private sectors together there were, by the early 1980s, over 3 million men who could retire with a full occupational pension before 65. Expressed another way, by the early 1980s, 40 per cent of all male workers in occupational pension schemes were entitled to a full occupational pension before 65 (House of Commons 1982).

In the private sector, although it is less common to find schemes with lower retirement ages, virtually all occupational pension schemes provide members with the right to an early retirement pension in cases of ill-health and inability to continue in work (Government Actuary 1979). It is also possible for an individual to opt to take early retirement, for his or her own reasons, but this usually means a substantial loss of potential pension income. However, where it is also in the interests of the firm for an individual to take early retirement either for staff-cutting purposes or because a reorganization is taking place, a company may use discretionary clauses in the occupational pension scheme to pay a full pension (Brown and Small 1985).

During the 1960s most British companies did not have a standard policy in their treatment of early retirement (McGoldrick 1982). From 1975 onwards, however, surveys of the National Association of Pension Funds show the increasing prevalence of early retirement arrangements on an established basis. By the 1980s nearly all schemes made specific provisions for employees to retire early voluntarily. In a survey of manufacturing establishments conducted in 1978–9, it was found that the use of early retirement by employers to manage reductions in manpower was widespread and the numbers retiring early were considerably increased when occupational pension schemes provided early retirement options. Carroll's (1990) survey of pension schemes found only two stating that early retirement was not available, but for only 47 per cent of schemes was it a *right* of the member. For the remainder, it was a discretionary benefit, helping to assist the employer in tailoring the size of the work-force to current needs.

A number of studies have confirmed that early retirement was used on a substantial scale by UK employers to achieve reductions in staffing (Institute of Manpower Studies 1983; 1987). However, one review of forty large organizations with well-established occupational pension schemes suggests that managers are becoming more sophisticated in their use of early retirement packages. There is a trend away from open-access early retirement schemes, towards targeted, closed-access schemes (see Chapter 6). Closed-access schemes are aimed at a target population, usually defined by type of job or specific individuals. They also tend to be associated with pruning staffing levels rather than wholesale rapid shutdown.

The job release scheme

In contrast to company provision for early retirement, public provision for early retirement via the government's job release scheme (JRS) has been mainly, in effect, for male manual workers (Bushell 1984). This scheme, which operated between 1977 and 1988, was a special temporary employment measure which allowed specific categories of older workers to retire early, on the condition that their jobs were filled by unemployed school leavers. No individual had the right to be able to join the scheme, acceptance depending on whether the employer would provide a new job for someone who was unemployed. Between 1977 and 1988 more than 250,000 individuals took advantage of JRS, 80 per cent of whom were males. Coverage of JRS was at a peak of 95,000 at 1 April 1984 but declined substantially thereafter. By June 1987 only 22,000 people were receiving JRS allowances (House of Commons 1989). This seems to be because JRS was restricted after 1 April 1984 to able-bodied men aged 64.

However, even during the period when the age-span of the scheme was greatest (in 1979–80), take-up by eligible men was only 12 per cent (Makeham and Morgan 1980). For the year 1983–4, when similar conditions of entry were applicable, a take-up rate of 6 per cent for women and 11 per cent for men was calculated (Bushell 1984). The

EC Labour Force Survey 1981 suggests that about 56,000 men aged 60–64 entered early retirement from the economically active during 1980–1. It also suggests that about 24,000 women entered early retirement during the same period. Of these new entrants probably one-third were JRS recipients as there were 25,000 new entrants to the JRS scheme in 1980–1 (Bushell 1984). In later years the importance of JRS was probably even greater as the number of new entrants to JRS rose to 49,000 in 1983–4. The bulk of this increase was due to a rise in the number of able-bodied men aged 62–64 taking early retirement. The numbers of women and disabled men entering the scheme actually declined in the period up to 1984.

Unlike pre-retirement benefits in a number of other countries, the allowance received with JRS was paid at a flat rate rather than earnings-related. This explains in part why take-up of the scheme was low and why the overwhelming majority of recipients were low-paid semi-skilled and unskilled workers (Bushell 1984). JRS was financially unattractive to people who were on above-average or average wages and who would not be able to supplement JRS with a pension from their employer (Makeham and Morgan 1980: 34). In 1983–4 69 per cent of successful applicants held occupational pensions, which perhaps explains why JRS applicants were over-represented in the public sector as in this sector manual workers are more likely to have an occupational pension than in the private sector.

The unemployment route

In the absence of alternative pre-retirement options to JRS, high numbers of older workers, mainly those from manual occupations (Laczko *et al.* 1988), have had to rely on unemployment benefit and means-tested income support in the years approaching state pensionable age. Since November 1981 all unemployed men aged 60 and over who have been out of work for over a year and who are entitled to income support claim the long-term rate and no longer have to register as unemployed. This measure was extended in 1983 to all unemployed men aged 60 and over irrespective of their duration of unemployment. By comparison there remains no special assistance for unemployed older women.

Another important change which came into effect in 1983 was the removal of the requirement for men aged 60 and over to register as unemployed in order to obtain contribution credits for the purposes of safeguarding their entitlement to a retirement pension when they reach 65. Retirement pension credits are now automatically awarded to fill any gaps in the contribution of men between the ages of 60 and

65, whether the gaps were due to low earnings or to unemployment. To some extent the unemployment rate of men aged 60–64 had been somewhat inflated because of this factor up until 1983. Between April and August 1983 162,000 older men were no longer included in the unemployment count. In July 1982 the unemployment rate of men aged 60 and over was 19.7 per cent. By July 1983 the rate had been halved to 9.6 per cent. Of those who were removed from the unemployment figures, it is estimated by the Department of Employment (Bushell 1984) that about 85,000 people had registered as unemployed to safeguard their contribution record. However, it cannot automatically be assumed that these people would not have taken a job if suitable employment were available. Earlier surveys of unemployed men in the 60–64 age group show that a high proportion were 'keen' to work (Donaldson 1979).

As unemployment has become increasingly prolonged, more and more unemployed older workers have ceased looking for work or at least have become less active job-seekers, but do not have formal retirement status. In 1983 42 per cent of unemployed women aged 50–59 who were receiving unemployment benefit were not actively looking for work (Laczko 1987).

It is not surprising that many unemployed workers give up looking for work, given their poor re-employment prospects. For example in 1985 a quarter of unemployed men aged 45 and over had not worked for three years or more. Of the latter, nearly half had not worked for five years (LMQR 1986). A significant proportion of older unemployed workers fall into the 'discouraged worker' category, that is they have given up looking for work because they believe there are no jobs. Table 4.1 examines the main reasons given by older unemployed workers in 1981 and 1983 for not seeking work. The most important reason given by over a quarter of men aged 50–59 was that 'they believed no jobs were available'. Roughly a quarter of men aged 60–64 also gave this reason but a somewhat higher proportion, around one-third, said that they were not looking for work because they considered themselves to be retired. A significant proportion of men aged 50–59 and 60–64 said that they were not looking for work because they were too sick to work (23 per cent and 16 per cent respectively).

Thus although these older men appear in the official UK unemployment figures which are based on the numbers of people receiving unemployment related benefits, their views suggest that they have left the labour force. Despite the fact that many may not be receiving occupational pensions and few will be receiving invalidity benefit, a substantial proportion seem to regard themselves as being sick/disabled or retired rather than unemployed or fall into the

Table 4.1   Older male claimants by reason not seeking work (percentages)

Reasons not seeking work	1981 50–59	1983 50–59	1981 60–64	1983 60–64
In paid job	11	11	5	7
Discouraged worker	29	28	27	24
Retired	8	10	33	33
Sick/disabled	22	23	15	16
Others*	26	23	9	13
	100%	100%	100%	100%
	(131)	(566)	(143)	(545)

Note: Percentages rounded.

* Includes those temporarily sick, waiting to start a new job and those on holiday.

Source: Labour Force Surveys 1981, 1983; own calculations.

'discouraged worker' category. In short, a high percentage of unemployed older workers have effectively exited from the labour force in the UK, with unemployment benefits themselves becoming a key measure facilitating early exit.

The disability route

In the UK, labour market 'chances' are not explicitly taken into consideration when invalidity benefit is awarded to older workers, as in some other European countries (for example Sweden and Germany). However, an increasing number of older workers on invalidity benefit have been leaving the labour market early in recent years, and a substantial part of the fall in the activity rates of older men is accounted for by a rise in the proportion defining themselves as disabled. In contrast to many other countries, an individual in the UK does not have to have a fixed level of disability before he or she can receive invalidity benefit. It is usually left to a doctor to judge whether they are incapable of working and to provide the relevant medical certificate. No doubt such judgements vary according to the labour market situation. Some research suggests, for example, that part of the increase in disability is attributable to the general rise in unemployment.

David Piachaud (1986), for example, examined data drawn from the Censuses of England for 1971 and 1981. The Census return provides self-reported information about self-defined economic positions, and therefore categories such as retired and disabled are not directly comparable with social security categories (for example people who say that they are retired could be receiving unemployment benefit). Piachaud found that in 1981, 6 per cent of men aged 55–59 and 11 per cent of men aged 60–64 fell into the disabled category: these were roughly double the proportions in 1971. Why has there been an increase in disability? Using census data for the forty-six counties of England, Piachaud related changes in disability, retirement and economic activity to changes in unemployment. He found that a substantial proportion of the overall increase in disability and the decline in economic activity is attributable to the increase in unemployment.

The evidence suggests that this is not because unemployment is directly the cause of the increase in disability. If it were the experience of unemployment itself that led to future disability, then it might be expected that disability would rise among younger men and women as well as among older men; this has not been the case. Piachaud shows that while the proportions of disabled have risen for all these age groups, the increases have been very much smaller than for older men. Therefore it would appear that as labour market conditions have deteriorated more older men have been seeking and have settled for the status of 'disabled'. In terms of the class background of these men, data from the General Household Surveys 1980–82 confirm that by far the majority (79 per cent) of men aged 60–64 who define themselves as sick or disabled were employed in manual occupations (Laczko *et al.* 1988). We also know that nearly all the men aged 60–64 who defined themselves as sick or disabled were receiving sickness or invalidity benefits (Laczko *et al.* 1988).

There are a number of advantages for the older individual in seeking disabled status. First, social security benefits for disabled people are higher than those received by unemployed people. In 1971 unemployment benefit was paid at the same rate as invalidity benefit; by 1981 disabled people received about one-third more (Laczko 1989: 159). Second, unemployment benefit is paid only for a year whereas invalidity benefit can be paid until age 70. Third, there may be less stigma associated with being classified as 'disabled' rather than 'unemployed'.

Early retirement or early exit?

We have outlined the early exit options that exist according to the benefits available to people who leave work early. The next major issue we have to consider is: what is the impact of these different routes on how people define their own status in late working life? Do they consider themselves retired, regardless of the particular benefits

Table 4.2   Older non-working men, by age and current status, 1979 and 1986 (column percentages, base = 000s)

	Aged 55–59		Aged 60–64	
	1979	1986	1979	1986
Unemployed	26.8	27.6	13.5	9.4
Discouraged	1.6	10.6	1.8	10.1
Long-term sick	53.8	36.7	30.1	34.2
Retired	11.7	13.1	49.6	36.4
Doesn't want job	0.9	4.8	1.1	5.7
Other, looking after home	5.2	7.4	3.0	4.3
All not employed	100.0	100.0	100.0	100.0
	(199,644)	(383,342)	(376,798)	(725,510)

Sources: Labour Force Surveys 1979; 1986; own calculations

they are receiving? Alternatively do we find different statuses and categories emerging, to match the range of options in terms of financial benefits? This is an area we shall explore in Chapter 5, where we examine in more detail the reasons people give for leaving work ahead of state pension age. In this chapter we summarize the key changes which developed from the late 1970s onwards, together with their relationship to the routes out of the labour force.

Tables 4.2 and 4.3 provide data from the British Labour Force Survey (LFS) for the period from 1979 to 1986. The LFS allows people no longer working to classify themselves into six groups: the unemployed (those without jobs but actively seeking work), the 'discouraged' (those not looking for work because they believe that no jobs are available), the long-term sick, the retired, those not wanting jobs, and 'others'. The tables show that even though the absolute number of older men and women defining themselves as retired has increased in recent years in Britain, the increase in those citing other reasons for not being in employment has been even greater. The inappropriateness of the 'early retirement' label with respect to older non-workers is apparent from Table 4.2, which shows that in 1986 only one in eight of men aged 55–59 and only just over one-third of men aged 60–64 categorize themselves as 'retired' (Casey and Laczko 1989).

A similar trend is apparent among women (Table 4.3). The proportion of women aged 55–59 not in employment who describe themselves as retired has declined somewhat since 1979 and was only 11 per cent in 1986. It is particularly striking that the proportion

Table 4.3 Older non-working women, by age and current status, 1979 and 1986 (column percentages, base = 000s)

	Aged 55–59		Aged 60–64	
	1979	1986	1979	1986
Unemployed	4.6	5.8	0.7	0.9
Discouraged	0.2	4.9	0.04	1.6
Long-term sick	9.3	16.8	2.2	7.0
Retired	13.3	10.9	64.0	50.2
Doesn't want job	0.6	20.5	0.1	15.1
Other, looking after home	72.1	41.0	32.9	24.7
All not employed	100.0	100.0	100.0	100.0
	(852,112)	(772,112)	(1,105,943)	(1,267,363)

Sources: Labour Force Surveys 1979; 1986; own calculations

of women aged 60–64 who say they are retired has dropped from 64 per cent to 50 per cent. Given that the absolute number of women outside of the labour force rose during this period much of this decline was relative. None the less, Table 4.3 does reveal the growing importance of other exit routes for older women. In particular there has been a significant rise in the proportion of older women leaving the labour force early who describe themselves as long-term sick or disabled. In 1979 9.3 per cent of women aged 55–59 came into this category compared to 16.8 per cent in 1986. As we saw at the beginning of this chapter, most of the early exit options that exist are primarily for men. Older women are less likely to have a good occupational pension, they are not able to claim the long-term rate of supplementary benefit, and JRS was open only to those women aged 59. Invalidity benefit may therefore provide an especially important means by which older women can leave the labour force early.

However, as expected, by far the majority of women aged 55–59 fall into the 'looking after home and other' category. This category has declined in relative importance since 1979. A large proportion of this category will include women who have never been employed. But among this group there are also women who have left the labour market early in order to care for a sick relative. As we show in Chapter 5, one in six women aged 55–59 who leave employment early do so in order to care for a relative in poor health. It is perhaps not surprising therefore that these women do not define themselves as retired. They may have retired from employment but they have not retired from work (again it is important to note that the peak age for informal care by women is between the ages of 45 and 64).

There is, in fact, a particular problem in applying the concept of retirement to women. Retirement most accurately describes what happens to men who leave paid employment in later life, but it is less useful in describing the experience of older women. Even at age 60, two-thirds of women who are not employed do not describe themselves as retired (Laczko 1989). It is not until age 65 that the majority of women describe themselves as retired, and even at age 74 only 56 per cent of women say they have retired (Table 4.4).

Equally apparent, however, is the inappropriateness of the characterization of older non-workers as unemployed. Only a quarter of men aged 55–59 and one-tenth of men aged 60–64 described themselves as 'unemployed' (Table 4.2). Despite the deterioration of the labour market, this proportion actually fell slightly for 60–64-year-olds between 1979 and 1986. However, among women aged 55–59 the proportion of unemployed rose somewhat from 4.6 per cent to 5.8 per cent (Table 4.3). Indicative of the growing number in the 55–64 age range with an indeterminate status is the rapid growth of the discouraged worker category, which accounts for 10 per cent of all older male non-workers in 1986 compared to well under 2 per cent in 1979. Among women aged 55–59, the proportion of discouraged workers was insignificant in 1979, but was almost 5 per cent in 1986. Also growing fast was the category of those claiming not to want a job, an insignificant proportion in 1979 but one in twenty of the older non-employed in 1986 (Casey and Laczko 1989). Among older women aged 55–59 the growth in this category has been even greater, rising from less than 1 per cent to over 20 per cent.

Social class and early exit

Although older manual workers are much more likely to leave employment early, they are less likely to describe themselves as early retired. For example, in the years 1980–82, 33 per cent of men in social classes I and II (professionals and managers) were not in paid employment, compared to 43 per cent of men in social classes V and VI (semi-skilled and unskilled). Yet only 13 per cent of men from social classes V and VI defined themselves as retired compared to 23 per cent of men in social classes I and II (see Table 4.5). Men in lower social classes have been disproportionately affected by the decline in older workers' employment opportunities. The same can be said of older women. In 1979 the proportion of older women, aged 55–59, in employment who were in manual jobs was 50.1 per cent, by 1986 the

Table 4.4 Economic status of women aged 50–74, by single years (percentages)

	Age																								
	50	51	52	53	54	55	56	57	58	59	60	61	62	63	64	65	66	67	68	69	70	71	72	73	74
Self-employed	4	5	3	4	4	3	3	3	3	3	2	2	3	1	1	1	1	1	1	1	1	0	0	0	1
Full-time employed	28	28	26	25	24	26	22	22	19	18	9	6	5	4	4	2	1	1	1	1	1	0	0	0	0
Part-time employed	28	28	29	27	27	21	23	22	20	18	12	14	11	10	9	5	5	4	4	3	2	2	1	1	1
Unemployed[1]	4	4	2	3	3	3	3	3	2	2	1	1	0	0	0	0	1	0	0	0	0	0	0	0	0
Looking after home	24	25	26	27	27	30	31	32	34	35	35	32	33	32	34	32	37	36	35	34	38	34	37	37	39
Retired	0	0	1	2	2	3	4	5	6	10	33	39	41	45	46	54	52	53	56	56	54	57	57	56	56
Long-term sick or disabled	3	3	4	3	4	5	5	5	6	6	0	0	0	0	0	0	0	0	0	0	0	0	0	0	0
Doesn't want a job	3	2	3	3	3	4	4	4	4	3	3	3	3	3	3	3	2	2	2	3	2	3	3	4	2
Discouraged[2]	1	1	3	1	2	1	1	1	2	2	1	1	0	0	0	0	0	0	0	0	0	0	0	0	0
Others[3]	6	4	4	5	3	4	4	4	4	3	4	3	4	4	3	2	1	2	2	2	3	3	1	3	1
Total (= 100%)	1,291	1,121	1,249	1,167	1,223	1,157	1,217	1,236	1,178	1,235	1,381	1,269	1,395	1,352	1,202	1,062	1,075	1,008	1,169	1,173	1,176	960	1,053	980	971

Notes: [1] Actively seeking work in reference week.
[2] Believe no jobs are available.
[3] Includes those on 'a government scheme', 'temporarily sick', on 'holiday' and 'waiting to start a job'.

Source: Labour Force Survey 1983; Laczko 1989

Table 4.5   Self-defined activity status of men aged 60–64, by socio-economic group (percentages)

	Non-manual		Manual		All
	Employers/ managers	Inter-mediate junior non-manual	Skilled	Semi-skilled and unskilled	
Employed	67	63	61	57	61
Retired	23	19	14	13	16
Unemployed	4	7	8	12	8
Permanently sick/ disabled	6	11	17	18	14
	100	100	100	100	100
	(435)	(334)	(829)	(557)	(2,155)

Source: General Household Survey 1980–2; own calculations

proportion had fallen to 43.5 per cent. These class differences reflect the fact that workers in lower social classes are more vulnerable to unemployment and are more likely to have poor health. They also (as noted in Chapter 3) have fewer opportunities to retire early on an occupational pension. In the case of women there has also been a continuing growth in service sector employment much of which includes lower-grade non-manual jobs.

Cross-national comparisons

In Chapter 1 we saw that the fall in the age of exit from the labour force has been as marked in Britain as in many other countries. What distinguishes Britain, however, is that fewer older workers who are not in the labour force describe themselves as retired in Britain than in other countries (OECD 1988a). The OECD has assembled data for ten countries in which people not in the labour force classify themselves either as retired or give some other reason for not seeking paid employment. In Britain among women aged 55–59, who were not in the labour force in 1981, only 9.4 per cent said they were retired. Although this figure rose to 11.6 per cent in 1986, it is still below that of all other countries except Australia and the USA. However, part of this could be explained by the fact that Britain has a lower pensionable age for women than in other countries. These figures underline again the difficulty involved in using the term early retirement to describe the way in which older women move out of employment into retirement.

Table 4.6 Proportion of retired among people not in the labour force[1]

	Year	Total			Males			Females		
		55–59	60–64	65+	55–59	60–64	65+	55–59	60–64	65+
Australia[2]	1983	14.7	32.8	43.6	60.2	76.5	86.9	2.8	7.2	13.0
	1985	14.5	33.0	44.9	51.5	76.0	86.5	2.8	7.8	15.5
Canada[2]	1971	4.7	13.8	42.0	34.2	59.4	87.6	1.1	2.8	12.2
	1981	20.2	35.4	62.6	20.6	31.3	68.3	19.9	38.0	58.6
	1985	24.1	40.4	67.4	22.8	37.1	74.0	25.1	42.6	62.8
Finland	1976	70.3	83.9	99.0	96.8	98.0	99.0	56.7	76.6	99.0
	1981	72.6	84.6	99.4	97.3	98.0	100.0	56.9	76.7	99.1
	1986	84.8	87.6	99.7	95.9	98.6	100.0	76.2	79.8	99.5
France	1971	26.0	44.9	72.2	79.8	90.0	98.4	9.7	24.9	56.7
	1981	25.3	60.8	79.6	67.4	91.7	98.9	10.4	39.7	67.5
	1986	33.9	69.3	80.7	69.0	94.5	99.4	16.1	49.7	68.7
Germany	1976	23.7	53.0	65.7	83.1	92.0	93.5	13.7	38.1	49.6
	1981	29.4	60.5	68.3	86.7	93.8	95.4	16.9	46.1	53.5
	1986	35.5	67.1	71.3	84.1	91.9	93.0	19.7	54.2	59.9
Norway[3]	1981	38.7	44.3	66.4	93.3	88.5	92.8	21.3	28.2	49.1
	1986	47.2	52.2	71.6	93.3	90.6	91.7	28.9	31.0	57.7
Portugal	1983	36.2	47.7	52.9	66.4	71.3	75.0	27.1	37.5	40.4
	1986	40.7	50.4	48.2	71.1	78.5	69.4	28.7	36.3	34.7

continued

Table 4.6—continued

	Year	Total			Males			Females		
		55–59	60–64	65+	55–59	60–64	65+	55–59	60–64	65+
Switzerland	1970	18.9	47.1	78.9	82.6	89.5	99.7	13.9	40.5	68.1
	1980	22.7	60.0	93.6	85.5	90.5	99.8	16.5	53.8	90.0
United Kingdom	1981	11.3	46.4	—	20.6	54.8	—	9.4	43.5	—
	1986	13.3	47.1	—	18.0	40.2	—	11.6	50.7	—
United States	1971	3.9	14.0	41.2	20.2	38.9	78.5	1.1	6.4	21.0
	1981	11.9	30.4	55.8	31.8	57.3	82.6	6.5	17.5	40.2
	1986	17.5	41.6	68.2	36.2	65.7	87.5	11.0	29.6	56.2

Notes: [1] In Australia, Canada, Finland, France, Norway, Switzerland and the United Kingdom 'retired' refers to self-declared major activity. In the United States, it refers to the main reason for not working among persons who did not work during the year. For Germany, 'retired' is classified according to pension income from previous labour force activity, including disability pensions.
[2] Includes the voluntarily inactive
[3] Includes the disabled

Sources: Australia: unpublished tabulations provided by the Australian Bureau of Statistics on the basis of the *Persons Not in the Labour Force Survey*

Canada: unpublished tabulations provided by Statistics Canada on the basis of the *Survey of Consumer Finances*

Finland: unpublished tabulations provided by the Central Statistical Office of Finland on the basis of the *Labour Force Survey*

France: unpublished tabulations provided by the National Institute for Statistics and Economic Studies (INSEE) on the basis of the *Labour Force Survey*

Germany: unpublished tabulations provided by the Statistical Federal Office on the basis of the *Mikrozensus*

Norway: unpublished tabulations provided by the Central Bureau of Statistics on the basis of the *Labour Force Survey*

Portugal: unpublished tabulations provided by the Ministry of Employment and Social Security on the basis of the *Labour Force Survey*

Switzerland: unpublished tabulations provided by the Federal Statistical Office on the basis of the *Census of Population*

United Kingdom: unpublished tabulations provided by the Department of Employment on the basis of the *Labour Force Survey*

United States: unpublished tabulations provided by the Bureau of Labor Statistics on the basis of the *Current Population Survey*

Source: OECD 1988a: 67

Table 4.6 shows that far fewer men aged 55–64 in the UK who were not in the labour force described themselves as retired than in other countries. Only 18 per cent of men aged 55–59 and 40.2 per cent of men aged 60–64 who were not in the labour force described themselves as retired in 1986. In all other countries except Canada, the comparable figures were much higher. For example in France 69 per cent of men aged 55–59 not in the labour force described themselves as retired in 1986.

Sources of income

One explanation for these cross-national differences may be related to the limited level of public and private provision for early retirement that exists in Britain. UK evidence suggests that older workers not in paid employment are more likely to describe themselves as retired when their main source of income comes from an occupational pension (Laczko et al. 1988). The most common source of income of men aged 60–64 describing themselves as retired was an occupational pension: nearly two-thirds of the manual early retired and over four-fifths of the non-manual early retired were receiving an occupational pension (Table 4.7). However, most men and women who leave work early rely on other sources of income for most of their income. Figures for 1983 for men aged 60–64 show that only 17 per cent of those not in employment were inactive occupational pensioners who were not receiving invalidity benefit, income support or the Job Release Allowance and were not unemployed. The most important benefits in 1983 were unemployment benefit (received by 32 per cent of men) and invalidity benefit (received by 28 per cent). Since 1983 the importance of long-term income support as a source of income for men who leave work early has increased substantially, while the importance of the Job Release Allowance has gradually declined.

Conclusion: changes in the meaning and significance of retirement

The evidence we have reviewed in this chapter would appear to support the argument that a new phase has been reached in the history of retirement. The surveys suggest that the transition between work and retirement is now becoming increasingly complex. The meaning and significance of retirement has changed, within the context of radical alterations to the character of employment. Increasingly, leaving employment in later life is not synonymous with the notion of

Table 4.7 Main sources of income of 'early retired', 'unemployed' and
'long-term sick' men aged 60–64, by class of last occupation (percentage
receiving any income from different sources)

	Early retired		Unemployed		Sick	
	Non-manual	Manual	Non-manual	Manual	Non-manual	Manual
Occupational pension	84	64	59	34	56	45
Long-term benefit*	28	36	10	5	92	84
Unemployment benefit	5	14	58	67	—	—
Supplementary benefit	3	9	20	31	8	9
N	(151)	(182)	(41)	(126)	(61)	(223)

Note: * Includes Disablement benefit, Invalidity benefit where the informant has
been off sick for over one year. Job Release benefits, Workmen's Compensation,
Invalid Wife Allowance, Attendance Allowance

Sources: General Household Survey 1980–2; own calculations; Laczko *et al.* 1988

retirement that developed in the immediate post-war period. Retirement has traditionally been viewed as withdrawal from the labour
market at a fixed age on a pension, receipt of which does not
necessarily prevent participation in the labour market (unlike JRS, or
the receipt of the long-term rate of income support). By contrast, the
retirement of many older people in recent years has yet to be
consolidated by societal norms: hence the ambiguity in the current
status of many older people who see themselves as being neither in
employment nor in retirement

Fewer people are now entering retirement from full-time work.
Many now experience a transitional phase, which may vary in length
from one to fifteen years. In 1986 half of men aged 55–59 who were not
in employment had not had a job for three years. Many older people
who are not in paid employment but who are below the state pension
age occupy an increasingly indeterminate status. This research, into
the way older people who are not in employment define their status,
has led us to question the appropriateness of using the term 'early
retirement' to describe what has been happening to older workers in
recent years. To talk about the fall in the activity rates of older workers
as being indicative of a trend to earlier retirement is potentially

misleading. Indeed, to use the term 'early retirement' to describe the phenomenon of falling participation rates is to grant it a legitimacy which it does not deserve. These arguments would suggest that the sociology of retirement is one of increasing complexity in the 1990s. In Chapter 5 we shall assess in more detail the main reasons people give when making the decision to leave work ahead of state retirement age.

5

The social consequences of early exit

Introduction

In Chapter 4 we examined some of the routes taken by people when moving out of the work-force in their fifties and sixties. In this chapter we review some of the reasons given by individuals for leaving work ahead of state retirement age. Knowledge of this area is valuable in giving us: first, a better understanding of the process of retirement, both in general and of early retirement in particular; second, it also provides a clearer grasp of the changes affecting older people at work. We are particularly concerned in this chapter to demonstrate the variety of influences which can affect an individual's decision to leave work and the impact it may have on their lives. We shall look at the reasons given by older workers for leaving work early: what sort of changes have been taking place in the 1980s? Are there, for example, significant variations according to class and gender? What are the trends in relation to income and health in respect of early exit?

In terms of the wider economic context, there is little doubt (as was noted in Chapter 4) that many early retirement options have been introduced primarily in response to labour market pressures. Research also indicates that older workers have been under social pressure to make way for younger people in the workplace (Bytheway 1986; Walker 1989). The House of Commons Social Services Committee, for example, noted in its report on flexible retirement in 1982 that

> It is not possible to explain the acceleration of the trend towards earlier retirement in the 1970s without reference to the recession. The strongest pressure comes from the high rates of youth employment leading to individual and collective belief that older workers should retire to make way for younger ones.
>
> (House of Commons 1982: vol. 1: 17)

This societal pressure may also be seen as part of a more general devaluation of the status and productive capacity of older workers, often seen in the form of age discrimination practices in employment (Laczko and Phillipson 1990).

The interpretation of individuals' stated reasons for leaving employment early must bear in mind this wider context of economic recession and 'ageism'. It is likely that, in a period of high unemployment and economic insecurity, the freedom of older workers to choose to remain in the labour force is effectively constrained; a decision to retire early may thus be a response to an uncertain future and insecurity in labour market prospects. In this situation, the distinction between 'voluntary' and 'involuntary' retirement is likely to become blurred, with only a minority of workers at either end of a continuum of 'absolute choice' and 'absolute compulsion'.

Research into early retirement

Research on why people leave work early falls into three main categories. First, there are nationally representative studies which have interviewed workers retiring before state pension age. An example here is the research carried out by the OPCS in the 1970s (Parker 1980). Second, there are studies which are concerned with one particular type of early retirement or early exit, often restricted to a particular locality or group of workers (McGoldrick and Cooper 1980; 1989; Makeham and Morgan 1980; Wood 1980; Walker 1985; Bytheway 1986; 1987; Schuller 1987). Third, there are findings from analysis of Labour Force Survey (LFS) data for the 1980s (Laczko et al. 1988; Casey and Laczko 1989; Laczko 1989). We shall examine the evidence from some of these studies regarding reasons given by older workers for leaving employment early. First, we focus on national and local studies of early retirement; second, the findings from this research are contrasted with the results from LFS data from the 1980s.

Research on early retirement: the experience of men

Before we consider some of the British research in this area, two observations might be made. First, there has always been some pressure to leave work before the age of 65, particularly from workers in manual occupations. Peter Stearns (1975) reports different groups of industrial workers in the 1890s pressing for a lowering of the retirement age (to 45 in mining and 55 in match manufacture). For these groups, proposals for a state pension at 65 (or 70 as originally the case in Britain) were seen as irrelevant to their needs – given the high rate of mortality in their particular industry. So the need to leave work early has always received some support. But the terms under which early retirement is experienced may be less than ideal. Workers may be unable to negotiate a time for early withdrawal which suits their individual needs. Indeed, early exit, if and when it comes, may be the result of external pressures (for example health problems, illness within the family), the effects of which have to be negotiated alongside the loss of work.

Results from American longitudinal research on retirement at different ages found that early retirees suffered more negative effects than people going at the age which was normal for their occupation. The research found that early retirees include many who are forced to retire because of poor health, age discrimination, or other involuntary reasons. These involuntary retirees outweigh those who retire voluntarily and so the average early retirement, it was argued, produces more negative effects (Palmore *et al.* 1985).

British research carried out in the 1970s suggested that ill-health was the major reason for early retirement among men (Parker 1980; Altman 1982). Altman, for example, analysed Family Expenditure Survey data from the 1970s and found that 70 per cent of the early retired were receiving health-related benefits. She concluded that 'most early retirement is not voluntary, but is forced upon people for health reasons' (Altman 1982: 358). This finding was confirmed in Parker's survey which found that of men who left work before the age of 60, 78 per cent gave ill-health as the main reason. Parker's research found that three-fifths of the early retired had some illness or disability which handicapped them or interfered with their activities in some way; this compared to one-quarter of people under pension age who were still working. Health reasons also played a major part in men's decisions as to whether to apply under the terms of the JRS. This was especially the case for manual workers. In the study by Makeham and Morgan (1980), 44 per cent of semi-skilled manual workers gave health-related factors as the principal reason for applying for JRS; the comparable figure for professional and managerial applicants was 21 per cent.

The implication of the above research would suggest, then, that health reasons are of major importance in explaining why people leave work ahead of state retirement age. But to focus on health alone would be an over-simplification. There are at least two explanations for this: first, the research by Altman and Parker was carried out before the participation rate of older workers had entered its sharpest point of decline. Hence, it is likely that these studies underestimated the influence of labour market factors in taking people out of the work-force. Second, early retirement was defined as a single category, with research failing to distinguish between the long-term sick and unemployed. In the case of Parker's study, for example, everyone over 55 years of age and not currently employed (or looking for work) is defined as early retired. Altman defined early retired men as 'all men recorded as being "unoccupied", "retired" or "sick or injured and not intending to work" and who were not engaged in any paid work' (Altman 1982: 356). Conflating different categories of early retired may have had the effect of masking any important variations, particularly across class and gender groups.

The OPCS study by Parker confirmed that for many categories of early retired, but particularly for those going for reasons of ill-health, considerable hardship could be experienced. A striking finding was the low average savings of the early retired – 73 per cent of men said that they had less than £2,500. The average amount of occupational pension received at the time of interview by just over half of the early retired men was £20 a week net. Almost one-third of the pensions were less than £10. Presumably many of these will be among those now experiencing considerable poverty as they enter late old age. Even at the time of interview, one-third of the early retired under pension age reported problems, most of which were related to financial difficulties (Parker 1980).

Financial considerations, along with health, will clearly be a major factor for many in terms of taking the decision whether to retire. This was highlighted in the study by McGoldrick and Cooper (1980; 1989; see also McGoldrick 1983), which focused upon early retirement among those in higher socio-economic groups. The first stage of the study was based on questionnaires and interviews with 120 male early retirees and their wives from companies based in the north west of England (McGoldrick 1983). Respondents had retired early under a wide variety of circumstances and very different levels of financial benefits. Types of early retirement included were Compulsory Early Retirement; Compulsory Early Retirement by request; Rundowns – Early Retirement instead of redeployment; Temporary Voluntary Early Retirement Schemes; Voluntary Early Retirement Schemes; Early Retirement by Choice. All had left their former company with early retirement terms arranged, either in the form of pension arrangements and/or severance payments. The main group excluded from the sample were those who had retired on complete disability grounds. The sample thus offers a considerable contrast to that of the national survey by Parker, where the majority of the early retired were not in receipt of company pensions and where those retiring on complete disability were included. In consequence, McGoldrick and Cooper offer a more optimistic view of the impact of early retirement. For the majority, in fact, financial inducements, plus the state of their own savings, played a dominant role in the retirement decision. A second important factor was a feeling expressed by many retirees that they 'had worked long enough' and that they deserved their retirement. One-third (34 per cent) expressed a need for more free time for hobbies, recreation or to spend with family; see also Makeham and Morgan (1980), who found that, for over a quarter of the professional and managerial applicants, wanting more leisure was the single most important reason for joining JRS. Third, a majority of those interviewed also mentioned a wide variety of problems affecting their work, such as changes in company structure; management; supervisory problems; shifts and unsocial hours, and stresses and strains of the job. Another important finding was that although the majority felt that they had not been pressured into the decision to retire early, certain pressures were experienced by retirees. The authors comment that 'some had felt influenced by company pressure or the feeling that they were not indispensable, pressure from unions or fellow workers and the belief that they were expected to retire to prevent younger workers being made redundant' (McGoldrick and Cooper 1980: 860). Finally, health factors were also important in the early retirement decision, with approximately half of those interviewed reporting that they had taken their health into consideration in some way.

These findings were further explored in the second stage of the research, a national postal survey of 1,800 early retired men (McGoldrick 1983; McGoldrick and Cooper 1989). This survey broadly confirmed the above findings, particularly in relation to the importance of finances. One of the authors summarized the results:

> The financial inducements received (75%) and the appropriateness of their own savings and finances (58%) had made it possible for them to consider the benefits of increased freedom and new activities. While some had felt pressures towards retiring, more importantly they had been influenced by their own positive perceptions of the potential of earlier retirement. A long-term belief in the benefits of retiring earlier was stated by 68% of respondents. . . .Their intentions with regard to time spending and lifestyle after retirement varied considerably, however. Whilst some sought time for relaxation and leisure, others looked for opportunities for self-development, community participation, or for further work or a new career.
>
> (McGoldrick 1983: 191)

Social class, along with gender, will be a major factor influencing the early retirement decision and the range of options open to the individual. Studies of individuals in particular industries and localities have helped illustrate this point, especially as regards the problems faced by those taking retirement from industries subject to structural decline. One such example is the research by Westergaard, Noble and Walker (1988) examining the effects of redundancy on a group of 370 workers employed in a privately owned steel company in Sheffield. Walker and his colleagues demonstrated the effect of redundancy in taking older workers out of the labour market, especially those who are close to state retirement age. They found, in fact, three years after experiencing redundancy, just one in four of those 55 and over were in work (excluding those who had retired at the normal pension ages). Walker (1989) has analysed in some detail the characteristics which distinguished the early retired from other older workers who remained actually or potentially in the labour market. The early retired were more likely to have been close to pension age, to report ill-health, to be better off financially, and to have non-manual occupations. However, Walker suggests that these supply-side characteristics do not give a complete explanation as to why people become early-retired. Walker notes that we must also take into account demand-side factors, in particular those which relate to changes in the demand for labour in national and local labour markets. In the Sheffield study, these factors included: first, the impact of redundancy from the steelworks; second, the level of demand for labour in the region and, in particular, the demand for labour for workers with specific skills; third, the lack of encouragement to employ older workers, a feature both of the local job centres and the wider economic and social context. Walker summarizes the findings of the research as follows:

> For the vast majority of older workers in the . . . study . . . it was likely to be the interaction of the two sets of influences – individual characteristics and knowledge about the demand for labour and their chances of securing further employment of a similar kind – that determined their response to redundancy. However, in the absence of financial security, the option of early retirement rested primarily on proximity to pension age.
>
> (Walker 1989: 86)

Leaving work early: the experience of women

The reasons why older women leave paid work ahead of state retirement age have received far less attention in comparison to that of men. There are at least two reasons for this: first, it reflects a common assumption that fewer women than men are in regular paid work and that, therefore, retirement is of less direct significance. However, according to the Labour Force Survey, by 1985 the proportion of women aged 50–59 in paid employment (55 per cent) was higher than the figure for men aged 60–64 (50 per cent) (LFS 1985). As a result of the sharp fall in the participation rate of older men, and the continuing growth in part-time employment among married women, gender differences in the employment rates of older men and women have been eroded. Thus it cannot be said that it is more normal for older women not to be employed than for older men. The main difference is that women and, in particular, married women, are more likely to enter retirement from part-time employment. Over half (53 per cent) of women aged 55–59 work part-time, although among unmarried women the proportion is much lower (33 per cent).

The concept of ageing is frequently defined in relation to labour-market status. The traditional concept of ageing for men is that 'old' is conterminous with 'non-employment'. Men move traditionally from full-time employment to full-time retirement. Women, however, are more likely to face a different kind of transition from employment to retirement, not because they are less likely to participate in the labour force, but because of their experience of part-time work outside the home. All this suggests not that retirement is not an issue for women, but that it raises different kinds of issues and pressures for them (Fennell *et al.* 1988; Hunt 1988).

The research that has been carried out suggests that women retire early for different reasons as compared with men. In 1976–7 two national surveys were carried out which included questions on reasons for giving up work in later life (Hunt 1978; Parker 1980). Although the age ranges were broader in the Hunt survey, and there were differences in the ways in which the data from the two surveys were analysed, the results were broadly similar (Parker 1982: 95). Health and redundancy were much less important reasons for women retiring under pension age than men (Parker 1980: 13). For example in Parker's study 69 per cent of men gave these two reasons compared to 44 per cent of women. Women on the other hand are more likely (according to Parker's evidence) to leave work early in order to care for a sick member of their family. Of women retiring between 45–59, 11 per cent gave this as their main reason for leaving their last job compared to only 3 per cent of men (see also Wright 1986; Hunt 1988; National Carers Survey 1990). Gender differences relating to exit from work were also identified in research on applications for the JRS. The JRS was open only to those women aged 59; only one-fifth

(50,000) of JRS recipients between 1977 and 1988 were women (Bushell 1984). A survey of JRS applicants in 1979 showed little difference between men aged 64 and women aged 59 in respect to reasons for applying for JRS (Makeham and Morgan 1980: 49). For example 27 per cent of men and 22 per cent of women gave personal ill-health as a reason. An important difference between men and women was that women were more likely to want to leave formal employment so that they could spend more time on unpaid work in the home, whereas men were more likely to say that they wanted more leisure time. This research also confirmed that a significant proportion of women (15 per cent) give up paid employment in order to look after a relative in ill-health.

Leaving work early: experiences in the 1980s

Most of the studies so far discussed focused on early retirement trends in the 1970s. However, results from the LFS suggest very different reasons for early withdrawal from the labour force during the 1980s. Analysis of these surveys indicate that labour market reasons – such as redundancy, dismissal, and early retirement under a company redundancy programme – are much more important reasons for early withdrawal from the labour force than ill-health (Laczko *et al.* 1988; Casey and Laczko 1989). Analysis of the Labour Force Surveys (LFS) permit us to distinguish between the different categories of people who leave employment early, based upon respondents' own definition of their status. This allows us to distinguish between reasons for early exit (that is all categories of persons not in employment) and reasons for early retirement (people who define themselves as early retired).

The LFS is a representative sample survey of people aged over 16 living in private households in Britain. It was conducted bi-annually from 1973 to 1983 and annually thereafter. In 1983 the response rate was 82 per cent (OPCS 1986). Data from surveys prior to 1979 are not comparable with later data and are by no means as extensive.

In the LFS information is available for older people no more than three years away from their last job. In the 1983 and 1986 LFS this meant that this question was applicable to only about one-half of all non-working men aged 55–64, although for some categories of persons this proportion was much lower (Laczko *et al.* 1988; Casey and Laczko 1989). For example in the case of men aged 60–64 who described themselves as retired, 72 per cent left employment more than three years before the survey and therefore were not asked their reasons for leaving their last job (see Table 5.1). This result,

Table 5.1   Older non-working men who left their last job more than three years before the survey, by age and current status (row percentages, base = 000s)

	Aged 55–59	Aged 60–64
Unemployed	40 (105,673)	37 (68,211)
Discouraged	66 (40,511)	65 (73,062)
Long-term sick	68 (140,426)	71 (247,879)
Retired	35 (50,070)	72 (471,092)
Does not want job	27 (18,219)	41 (41,257)
Other	47 (28,639)	48 (31,096)
All not working	52 (38,334)	57 (725,510)

Sources: Labour Force Survey 1986; Casey and Laczko 1989

incidentally, contradicts the findings of other research where it is suggested that 'early retirement tends to be within two or three years of normal retirement for the bulk of workers retiring early' (Institute of Manpower Studies 1987: 35).

Table 5.2 is based on analysis of the 1983 Labour Force Survey and refers to all non-working men aged 60–64. The Table shows that of those men aged 60–64 who left employment between 1980 and 1983, 29 per cent were made redundant or dismissed and 32 per cent left because their employer introduced an early retirement scheme as part of a company redundancy programme. Although we do not know how far older workers welcomed opportunities to leave work early under schemes of the latter type, Table 5.2 does cast some doubt upon the extent to which the decision to leave work early was voluntary. In the majority of cases, men who left employment during this period might not have done so if there had not been an economic recession (see also Walker 1989).

Contrary to findings from research discussed earlier, ill-health is not a major reason for leaving work early – only 14 per cent of men cited this reason. A more important reason than ill-health, given by 21 per cent of respondents, was that they had 'retired' (that is they had reached the normal age for retirement in their occupation). Those falling into this category include the many people who are employed in occupations which have lower retirement ages than the state pensionable age. It is not necessarily the case, however, that all these people actually chose to retire before 65. For example it is possible that these older workers were under greater pressure to retire at the normal age for their occupation than might otherwise have been the case had labour market conditions been different.

Table 5.2   Non-employed men aged 60–64, by reason for job loss and current status 1983 (percentages)

Reasons for jobs loss	Aged 60–64
Redundancy/dismissal	29
Early retired when employer cut back on staff	32
Ill-health	14
Retired – normal age for occupation	21
Other	4
Total	100
	(887)

Sources: Labour Force Survey 1983; own calculations

The LFS also shows that we need to be careful in reducing the 'non-working population' of older people to either unemployed or early retired. This point is brought out in Table 5.3 which refers to non-employed men aged 60–64 in the four self-defined categories by age, sex, and social class summarized in Chapter 4. The four categories are the unemployed (people who were actively seeking work in the survey week); the retired; the long-term sick and disabled; and the 'discouraged' (people who have given up looking for work because they believe no jobs are available). It might be argued that the categories the LFS offers non-workers to describe themselves are somewhat fluid. For example how a non-employed person chooses to describe themselves is likely to depend very much on the nature of the question asked (Casey and Laczko 1989). However, it has been established that these categories do correspond with benefit categories (Laczko *et al*.1988). Most of those calling themselves 'long-term sick' do indeed receive invalidity benefit. Those calling themselves 'unemployed' are more likely to be receiving unemployment benefit and those calling themselves 'retired' are more likely to be receiving an occupational pension. As expected, by far the majority of the unemployed and 'discouraged' left their last job because of redundancy/dismissal, or because they left work under a company early-retirement programme designed to avoid redundancies (see Table 5.3). However, labour market reasons are also important for other groups, including those describing themselves as early retired and long-term sick.

The main difference between the early retired and unemployed/discouraged in Table 5.3 is that the early retired are much more likely

Table 5.3 Reason left last job:* men aged 60–64 not in paid work, by class of last job (percentages)

Reasons	Early retired	Sick	Un- employed	Dis- couraged	All
Non-manual					
Redundancy/ dismissal	3	14	58	63	19
Early retired when employer cut back on staff	47	26	17	26	37
Ill-health	3	49	3	0	9
Retired – normal age for occupation	43	7	5	5	28
Other	4	4	17	6	6
Total	100 (295)	100 (72)	100 (81)	100 (38)	100 (486)
Manual					
Redundancy/ dismissal	14	23	78	68	36
Early retired when employer cut back on staff	62	13	8	15	31
Ill-health	3	60	3	3	19
Retired – normal age for occupation	20	1	—	1	8
Other	1	3	11	13	5
Total	100 (352)	100 (230)	100 (194)	100 (101)	100 (887)

Note: * Asked of those who left work up to three years before the survey

Source: Labour Force Survey 1983; Laczko *et al* 1988: 324

to have left work as part of a company redundancy programme rather than because of dismissal or redundancy. Within the early retired group there is, however, a marked difference between manual workers and non-manual workers. Three-quarters of manual workers gave labour-market related reasons for leaving their last job compared to half of non-manual workers.

Early exit and ill-health

Table 5.3 also reveals that ill-health is a much less significant reason for those who define themselves as retired. Only 3 per cent of the older men aged 60–64 who saw themselves as retired gave ill-health as the main reason for leaving their last job. The reason for this is that men who are long-term sick and receiving invalidity benefit do not call themselves early retired in the LFS. In previous studies the long-term sick were included in the early retired population (Parker 1980; Altman 1982). However, while this factor may explain in part why ill-health seems to be an insignificant reason for early retirement in the LFS, it cannot be the main factor. Even when we define early retirement more broadly, ill-health is still not a major reason for leaving work early. This is not to say however that men who leave employment early are not in poor health. Analysis of General Household Survey (GHS) data, for example, shows that the early retired were somewhat more likely than the employed in their age group to report a long-standing illness, yet few early retired men gave this as a reason for leaving their last job (Laczko et al.1988). The apparent discrepancy between early retirees' reasons for giving up work early and their somewhat poorer health may be explained by the fact that older men in ill-health tend to be targeted by companies wishing to reduce manpower. It is evident that many companies design 'voluntary' redundancy and early retirement schemes to attract those in poor health, and those regarded as least productive (Daniel and Stilgoe 1978; Institute of Manpower Studies 1983).

This point is also suggested in Table 5.3. Among men defining themselves as long-term sick there is evidence to suggest that labour market factors have been important in influencing their decision to leave employment early. Over one-third of men from manual occupations and two-fifths of men from non-manual occupations, who defined themselves as long-term sick, said that the main reason why they left their last job was not because of ill-health but because of dismissal, redundancy or because their employer was using early retirement to cut back on staff (Laczko et al.1988).

As noted in Chapter 2, older male manual workers who are not in employment are considerably more likely to define themselves as unemployed or sick than retired. This evidence alone suggests that many older male manual workers have been forced to leave work early either because of ill-health or redundancy. This is confirmed by analysis of reason for leaving last job by social class. In general, manual workers are much more likely to have left the labour force because they were made redundant or dismissed (36 per cent), or because of ill-health (19 per cent). The corresponding percentages for non-manual workers are 19 per cent and 9 per cent. Non-manual workers were much more likely to report that they had 'retired' (28 per cent) and were also somewhat more likely to have left work early under a company redundancy programme (37 per cent). The respective figures for manual workers are 8 per cent and 31 per cent.

Changes in early exit during the 1980s

Figures from the 1986 LFS show a similar picture with respect to reasons for leaving employment for the period 1983–6, except that health reasons seem to be more important and early retirement under a company redundancy scheme, relatively less important (see Table 5.4). Comparing results from 1983 with those from the 1986 survey is difficult because of changes in the wording of questions between these two periods. Table 5.4, which shows the reasons why non-employed men aged 60–64 left their last job, suggests that over the period 1983–6 early retirement under a company redundancy programme may have become less significant. In 1983 32 per cent of all men not in employment gave this reason for leaving last job compared to only 16 per cent in 1986. Such a change might be expected, given that unemployment rose much more sharply in the period 1980–3 than during 1983–6. However, in 1983 people leaving employment under JRS were not identified and it could be the case that the 8 per cent of men giving JRS as a reason for leaving work (see Table 5.4) were counted as people retiring under a company redundancy programme in 1983. But this would not account for all of the difference between 1983 and 1986. There seems therefore to have been some slow down in the proportion of men leaving work early under early retirement schemes introduced as part of company redundancy programmes in more recent years.

Among men aged 55–59 who are not in employment we only have data on reasons for leaving last job for 1986 (see Table 5.4). However, the impact of labour market factors on their decision to leave work early seems to be even more important than among men aged 60–64. Table 5.4 shows that nearly two-thirds of non-employed 55–59-year-olds left employment between 1983 and 1986 because of redundancy or dismissal (including a temporary job coming to an end) or early retirement as part of a company redundancy programme. The corresponding figure for men aged 60–64 was about half. This difference is to be expected given that 38 per cent of men not in employment aged 55–59 are unemployed/discouraged compared to 19.5 per cent of men aged 60–64. Moreover, men aged 55–59 have

Table 5.4   Reason left last job:* men aged 50–59, 60–64 and women aged 50–59 not in paid work in 1986

	Men		Women	
	_50–59_	_60–64_	_50–59_	_60–64_
Redundancy/dismissal	39	23	19	7
Temporary job which came to an end	8.4	3.5	8	2
Resigned	3	2	10	4
Early retired when employer cut back on staff	15	16	7	2.5
Early retirement under job release scheme	2	8	2	3
Health reasons	19	21	22.5	3
Retired – normal age for occupation	5	21	9	65
Family/personal reasons	1	2	15	6
Other reasons	7	3	3	2
No reply	0.4	0.3	0.8	0.4
	100	100	100	100
	(197,469)	(311,158)	(318,535)	(271,098)
	333,350	414,392	1,004,188	996,770

Notes: * Never had a job or left last job three years before survey. Asked of those in employment up to three years before the survey. Figures may not add up to exactly 100% because of rounding.

Sources: Labour Force Survey 1986; unpublished figures from Department of Employment

fewer opportunities than men aged 60–64 to retire early voluntarily as there tend to be fewer occupations with a retirement age below 60. Thus twice as many men aged 60–64 report that they have 'retired' from their last job compared to 10 per cent of men aged 55–59.

Leaving work early: the experience of women

Table 5.4 shows that nearly one-quarter (24 per cent) of non-employed women aged 50–59 in 1986 left paid employment in the three years before the survey. The results confirm the findings of earlier studies in showing that women are much more likely to leave employment for family or personal reasons. In 1986 15 per cent of women aged 50–59 gave this reason compared to 2 per cent of men aged 60–64, and 1 per cent of men aged 50–59. Women still provide most of the informal care in the community, and women in this age group may be withdrawing from employment to look after a sick husband or elderly relative. But the main reasons why women leave the labour force early relate to labour market factors and their own ill-health. In terms of the former, Table 5.4 shows that about one-third of women gave up their last job involuntarily, either because of redundancy/dismissal, a temporary job came to an end or because their employer was cutting back on staff. However, the findings of the importance of health factors are particularly striking. Indeed, ill-health is the most important single reason given by women for leaving last job. Over one-fifth (22.5 per cent) of women aged 50–59 gave this reason. Ill-health would appear to be a relatively more important reason for older women than for older men. This is consistent with the higher rates of morbidity displayed by women in all age groups. However, an added factor may be that women, faced with a range of duties within the home, are forced to give a higher priority to this area than to work outside the home. Another factor (as noted in Chapter 4) is that women have fewer options than men in terms of routes out of the labour market. First, women are less likely to have a good occupational pension, or indeed any occupational pension in comparison with men. Second, special schemes such as JRS were mainly restricted to men. Third, older unemployed women have not been able to draw the long-term rate of income support, again in contrast to older men. Finally, if unemployed, women are also less likely to be eligible for means-tested income support because of their spouse's earnings. Thus for women *de facto* retirement on invalidity benefit is one of the few options they have left if they wish to leave the labour force before age 60. What is not clear is how far reasons of ill-health are related to labour market factors. LFS data give us some indication of why people leave employment but tell us little about the factors that may be preventing their re-employment. Is it the case, for example, that women who become ill find it increasingly difficult to return to employment and therefore continue to receive invalidity benefit? Evidence from Sweden suggests that a rising number of older women have been retiring early on disability pensions during the 1980s because they are unable to obtain jobs (Laczko and Walker 1985). A similar pattern may also be at work in the UK.

Poverty and early exit

A major issue in terms of the impact of early retirement will be the effect it has on levels of income. Evidence on this issue comes from a study of GHS data for the period 1980–2 (Laczko et al.1988). The poverty line used in the study was the long-term rate of income support (formerly supplementary benefit) which is payable to elderly people, and which is the definition of poverty most often used in UK studies concerned with assessing pensioner poverty. Those with incomes up to 140 per cent of this level are conventionally considered to be on the margin of poverty. To allow for the fact that incomes were being compared over a three-year period, the scale rate for 1981 was taken as the poverty line as this figure approximates to the median rate for these three years.

Before outlining the findings of the research a few comments should be made about the limitations of the research. First, supplementary benefit scale (now income support) rates are defined exclusive of housing costs; if these were included the poverty line would be more generous. Thus in this respect the study under-estimates the level of poverty. Second, the GHS provides only gross income data for those not in paid employment, and in this respect it under represents, to a limited extent, the proportion of people on low incomes. Third, because of the difficulty of generating a large enough sub-sample of people who had left employment early, the analysis was confined to married men. Again this is likely to under-estimate the extent of poverty because, as previous research on the resources of elderly people suggests, married couples are less likely to experience poverty than single people (Ermisch 1982: 42).

In 1981 the long-term rate of supplementary benefit for a couple was £47.35 per week, and those with incomes up to 40 per cent above this level were receiving between £47.36 and £66.26 per week. Table 5.5 provides a comparison of the incomes of married men aged 60–64 who defined themselves as employed, retired, long-term sick, or un-employed. These categories are divided according to whether the respondent's last job was manual or non-manual. If we consider the retired, long-term sick, and unemployed as 'non-employed' we find that altogether 13 per cent of the non-manual non-employed and 25 per cent of the manual non-employed had incomes on or below the poverty line. A further 12 per cent of the non-manual non-employed and 29 per cent of the manual non-employed had incomes up to 40 per cent above the poverty line. Within the non-employed group (see Table 5.5), we find as expected that the unemployed have the lowest incomes. The percentage of the unemployed from manual occupations below the poverty line is 37 per cent compared to figures of 20 per cent and 23 per cent among comparable groups of the retired and sick.

In general the non-employed were much more likely to have low incomes than the employed. For example only 5 per cent of the

Table 5.5 Distribution of weekly gross income: currently employed, early retired, unemployed, and sick men aged 60–64 and their wives, by class (row percentages)

	1981 long-term SB* level				Median income	
	SB level or less (1)	Up to 40% above SB (2)	More than 140% of SB (3)			
Non-manual					%	£
Employed	9	4	87	100	168	(264)
Early retired	8	11	81	100	105	(88)
Unemployed	23	9	68	100	92	(22)
Sick	21	15	64	100	76	(33)
All non-employed	13	12	75	100	100	(143)
Manual						
Employed	5	4	91	100	121	(441)
Early retired	20	28	52	100	68	(98)
Unemployed	37	29	34	100	57	(65)
Sick	23	30	47	100	63	(98)
All non-employed	25	29	46	100	63	(261)

Notes: * SB = Supplementary Benefit
    (1) £47.35 p.w.
    (2) £47.36 p.w.–£66.26 p.w.
    (3) Above £66.26 p.w.

Source: General Household Survey 1980–82; Laczko *et al.*, 1988

manual employed men had incomes on or below the poverty line. The median gross income of the manual early retired (£68) was only 56 per cent of the median income of the manual employed (£121). This would suggest that in general early retirement entails a substantial loss of income.

However, Table 5.5 does highlight that a small proportion of older men do 'earn their poverty', that is there is poverty among older men in employment. The significance of this is that some older men in paid employment who are on low incomes are likely to experience a relatively small drop or perhaps no fall in income, when moving from employment to retirement. Unfortunately the data from the GHS provide no indication of how much income a particular individual has lost after leaving employment. We cannot compare income before and after retirement with cross-sectional data from the GHS. However, other research which has focused on people leaving work early under the JRS suggests that for some low-paid individuals, leaving the labour force early entails relatively little loss of income. The Job Release Allowance was found to be a good substitute for the wages of unskilled and semi-skilled workers (*Employment Gazette* July 1980: 724).

For some individuals the prospect of retiring on a low income may be more desirable than the prospect of continuing to work for low pay in an arduous occupation. In the case of these people it is difficult to argue that retirement creates more dependency (see also Kohli 1988; Johnson 1989a).

Explaining poverty

Poverty in early retirement, as in retirement generally, is closely related to occupational status prior to leaving work (Townsend 1979). The poverty of the older non-employed, like the poverty of elderly people, needs to be seen in the context of their previous labour market position. People who are in low-paid or insecure employment, who have not been able to accumulate savings or who cannot expect to retire on a good occupational pension, are more likely to experience poverty in later life. Avoiding poverty in old age requires having other sources of income and/or having a history of stable employment in a well-paid job. Poverty in old age has been shown to be primarily a function of low economic and social status prior to retirement and secondly the relatively low level of state benefits (Walker 1986: 209). Findings from the GHS with respect to the sources of income of the older non-employed confirm this analysis. The poorest of the older non-employed are those who are most reliant on state benefits and have little income from other sources. Table 5.6 shows that roughly two-thirds of the average gross income per week of 'poor' early retired couples (incomes below 140 per cent of the supplementary benefit level) comes from state benefits. By contrast early retired couples with incomes above 140 per cent of the supplementary benefit level received less than one-quarter of their income from state benefits.

Avoiding poverty in early retirement entails having other sources of income, in particular an occupational pension but also unearned income from property, savings and investments, and income from a spouse who is in paid employment (see Table 5.6). The most important single source of income for early retired men with incomes above the 140 per cent of supplementary benefit level was an occupational pension. Nearly 90 per cent of men in this latter category

Table 5.6   Comparison of 'poor' and 'non-poor' early retired married men aged 60–64 with no dependants (percentages)

	Poor[1]	Non-Poor[2]
Percentage of average gross income per week from different sources		
Occupational pension	24	44
State benefits	65	23
Unearned income	9	17
Wife's Earnings	2	16
	100	100
Percentage receiving an occupational pension		
	48	87
Percentage with wife in paid work		
	12	29
N	(62)	(126)

Notes: [1] Up to 140% of 1981 SB* long-term rate for couples
         [2] Over 140% of 1981 SB long-term rate for couples
         * SB = Supplementary Benefit

Sources: General Household Survey 1980–2; Laczko *et al.* 1988.

were receiving an occupational pension. By contrast only 48 per cent of early retired men with incomes below 140 per cent of the supplementary benefit level had an occupational pension.

Even those older manual workers who are members of occupational pension schemes are often at a disadvantage because schemes often base their calculation of the pension on the final year's salary of the individual. This results in a lower level of benefit for manual workers whose earnings tend to decline past middle age.

Long-term consequences of leaving employment early

While the proportion of elderly people in poverty in Britain remains high, especially compared to some other OECD countries (Hedstrom and Ringen 1987), the overall position of elderly people, and the average income of elderly people has shown some improvements (Child Poverty Action Group 1987). But what will be the effect of the fall in the age of exit from the labour force on income poverty in old age? Is there a danger that the rapid increase in early exit that has occurred will have the effect of producing a cohort of poorer elderly people, thereby decreasing the relative average income of elderly people and increasing inequality within this age group?

Income from employment has been a declining source of pensioner income for a number of years and yet the average income of elderly people has been improving. Why, then, should we expect that a further decline in income from employment to affect adversely elderly people's income? The answer lies in the pattern of early exit that has developed in recent years in this country, which we discussed in Chapter 4. There is evidence that over the long term, the growth of retirement was linked to the spread of occupational pensions, but this can hardly explain the recent sharp growth in early exit. Since 1971 there has been relatively little growth in the number of people covered by occupational pension schemes. As we have seen, a large proportion of people who retire early at the present time do not have good occupational pensions.

Those who are likely to be most vulnerable in the future are the older workers who are currently long-term unemployed. They have interrupted contribution records, few opportunities to save for old age, and little prospect of re-employment. These people will enter retirement with fewer resources than earlier cohorts even though they will spend a longer period in retirement. Furthermore, although women have been less directly affected by the growth of early exit, the early exit of their husbands could exacerbate their vulnerability to poverty in old age. Because of the significance of retirement in precipitating low incomes and poverty, distance from finishing work (that is since leaving full-time employment) is also a key factor in creating deprivation (Walker and Laczko 1982: 215). Research across a number of countries has shown that length of time since last employment is an important factor in the incidence and depth of poverty among the very elderly (see Shanas *et al.* 1968). The combination of increased life expectancy and earlier exit from the labour force means that many more older people can expect to live on pensions and related benefits for much longer than ever before. In later years financial problems can arise as savings dwindle, houses fall into disrepair and the purchasing value of occupational pensions decreases (unless fully indexed).

It is difficult to quantify with cross-sectional data, the extent to which early exit might accentuate inequality of income in old age. A rough comparison of the incomes of older non-employed men aged 60–64 and older retired men aged 65–69 was made using GHS data for 1980–82 (Laczko 1989). This comparison is somewhat crude, because it was not possible to exclude from among the retired aged 65–69 people who had left employment early but had now reached state pensionable age. The comparison suggests that there is greater income inequality within the older non-employed population than within the retired population. This is perhaps not surprising, given that the older non-employed group includes at one extreme the long-term unemployed, and at the other, people who are quite wealthy and who have chosen to give up work early because they can afford to. The important point to note from this comparison is that a substantial proportion of older people who have left work early are poorer than the retired. For example one-quarter of men aged 60–64, from manual jobs who were non-employed, had a weekly income on or below the supplementary benefit poverty line, compared to 19 per cent of retired men aged 65–69. This would suggest that the trend towards early exit is likely to exacerbate income poverty in old age because early exit tends to be concentrated upon lower-income manual workers.

Conclusion

The LFS has the advantage of being nationally representative, and provides data for the whole early exit population. But as we have seen we are able to investigate only a limited number of main reasons for early exit. The picture that emerges from our analysis, however, is that the majority of older men might not have left the labour force early in the absence of an economic recession. The importance of labour market factors in the exclusion of older workers from the labour force is even greater when the barriers to the re-employment of older workers are taken into consideration. In Chapter 6 we shall consider the reasons given by employers and the state for encouraging early retirement: did it result in positive gains for individual firms? Did it result in younger people being offered more jobs as a result of older people leaving work early? What lessons can be drawn from the use of early retirement options for organizations and individuals in the 1990s?

6

The implications of early exit for the labour market

Introduction

This chapter is concerned with the implications of current patterns of early exit from the labour force for enterprises and the labour market. In the first part of the chapter we consider the implications of early exit at the micro-level of individual firms and enterprises. Here we assess the advantages and disadvantages for organizations that use early retirement. We also consider any lessons that might be learnt from the experience of using early retirement options over the past ten years. Then, the broader impact of early exit is examined. We consider in particular how far early exit has reduced unemployment, particularly among younger workers. The final part of the chapter looks to the future and the long-term implications of early retirement in the changing labour market of the 1990s. Is the early retirement trend so well established that it will continue even if unemployment falls and a shortage of young workers becomes apparent? How likely are employers to respond favourably to incentives from the state to retain or employ more older workers in the future? The first task, however, is to look at what we know about the costs and benefits to enterprises using early retirement options.

Implications for organizations

Despite the substantial growth in early retirement in recent years, very few organizations in the UK seem to have conducted serious cost-benefit analyses of the implications of early retirement policies (Institute of Manpower Studies 1983). The main recent UK evidence concerning employers' use of early retirement comes from two surveys carried out by the Institute of Manpower Studies (IMS) and from government evaluation of the job release scheme (JRS).

The first IMS survey, conducted in 1983, covered a sample of fifty UK employing organizations, both large and small, and including manufacturing and services. However, this sample was selected in such a way as to be representative of a variety of early retirement practices and is not a representative sample of employing organizations. There is a bias within the sample towards those enterprises which had implemented early retirement schemes since 1979, and organizations with some experience of flexible retirement and phased retirement. It should also be added that only representatives of management were interviewed. No employee representatives or older workers were asked about early retirement practices in their organizations.

In the second survey (IMS 1987), the IMS researchers returned to twenty-six of the organizations in the first survey in order to consider how their policies and practices had developed since that time. A further fourteen organizations were added to the original group. The total sample of forty organizations were all large with well-established occupational pension schemes covering a high proportion of their work-force. Neither study included organizations which were making use of the JRS at the time of the survey. It is important to point out, therefore, that the enterprises in the IMS surveys were under no obligation to replace older workers taking early retirement with new employees.

The advantages of early retirement

In looking at the effects of early retirement on the enterprise, we would make a distinction between, first, firms that use early retirement primarily in order to reduce staffing levels, and second, those using early retirement to change the composition of their work-force. Evidence from the IMS surveys suggests that reduction of staffing levels is the dominant rationale for early retirement. The IMS research also shows that since 1979, the use of early retirement to reduce staffing has increased dramatically in those organizations with occupational pension schemes and which have an ageing work-force. As a means of reducing staff, selective voluntary early retirement was favoured because it avoided the industrial relations implications of both compulsion and redundancy, while permitting a greater degree of management control than either reliance on non-replacement of natural wastage or the last-in-first-out restriction of compulsory redundancy (IMS 1983). By using early retirement, employers can design schemes to attract those who are regarded as both less productive and more expensive to employ. It should be stressed, however, that employers are able, and can afford to, offer early retirement, only where employees are entitled to an occupational pension and have accrued significant pension rights under the terms of such a scheme. The costs of early retirement are, in fact, considerable. They are usually met in large part by employers who compensate the pension fund for the earlier and thus longer-than-anticipated payments it will now make to early retirees. It is necessary for an individual to have accrued significant pension rights in order to make enhancement of an early pension affordable for the firm. Older individuals will also not volunteer for early retirement if they have not accrued sufficient pension rights. Given these factors early retirement has more limited applicability in small enterprises where occupational pension schemes are less likely to exist (IMS 1983).

As noted before, employers also have less scope to use early retirement to reduce the number of older manual workers and female workers in their work-force as these workers are less likely to have an occupational pension or if they do have such a pension it is more likely to be too low to finance early retirement (IMS 1983). Accordingly, 'Blue collar employees cannot generally afford to retire early, even with the actuarial reduction removed. Their potential pension is simply not large enough and most such employees feel the need to continue working as long as possible' (IMS 1987).

Manual workers are likely to have a lower level of accrued pension rights (as a result of relatively recent entry to such schemes, voluntary membership, a lower contribution rate to the scheme and a generally shorter length of service than non-manual workers). Women are disadvantaged in respect of occupational pensions because of their broken pattern of fund membership and a lower level of accrued pension rights than males (IMS 1983). In sum, this form of early retirement, where employers enhance occupational pension rights, tends to be used to reduce staffing levels in larger enterprises and is most useful in reducing manpower among older male white-collar employees. The advantage of this form of early retirement is that it provides employers with a socially acceptable means of effectively dismissing older non-manual workers.

However, (as noted in Chapter 3) there is also evidence that early retirement is increasingly being used in a more sophisticated and selective fashion in order to enable employers to restructure and rationalize their labour force. There is a clear trend towards targeted, closed-access schemes, particularly in the service sector. The advantage of closed-access as opposed to open-access schemes is that they allow employers to maximize their control over who should be offered early retirement by restricting early retirement to certain categories of persons. By enhancing their control over the early retirement process, employers are able to minimize the costs to their firm. Such closed-access arrangements are frequently used by employing organizations for promoting internal promotion for younger workers and in aiding organizational and technological change (IMS 1987).

Evidence for the advantages of early retirement may also be cited from research on the JRS. Research by Bushell in the early 1980s suggested that 61 per cent of employers who accepted applications to JRS during 1982–3 perceived advantages in the JRS for their organization (Bushell 1984). The major advantages were seen to be the replacement of older with younger staff, enabling older staff to retire early if they wished, the replacement of staff who were sick, and the contribution which JRS might make to organizational flexibility. Thus JRS enabled enterprises to restructure and rejuvenate their work-force. Figures for entrants to JRS in 1982–3 show that in cases of direct replacement the pay of replacement workers was less on average, than that of early retirees. Enterprises were therefore able to make savings on salary costs by replacing low-paid older workers by even lower-paid younger ones (Bushell 1984). However, these savings to the enterprise might have been considerably greater, albeit at the cost of greater expense to the state, if the JRS scheme had been more financially attractive to better paid employees. JRS benefits are paid at a flat-rate and tend to be too low to be financially attractive to people who are on above average or average wages and who would not be able to supplement JRS with a pension from their employer (Makeham and Morgan 1980: 34).

JRS recipients tend to be over-represented among persons from semi-skilled and unskilled occupations (Bushell 1984: 16). In 1978 over 51 per cent of JRS beneficiaries had been employed in semi-skilled and unskilled occupations. This may have been considered as an advantage by many employers because it enabled them to offer early retirement to older manual workers from semi-skilled and unskilled occupations, who might otherwise not have been able to retire early under a company early retirement scheme for the reasons noted above. It enabled them to rationalize and restructure their older work-force with less likelihood of losing skilled personnel. Employers using JRS probably had less control over the selection of early retirees than in enterprises developing their own early retirement schemes. But unlike employers using their own early retirement schemes, employers using the JRS had greater scope to offer early retirement to older manual workers.

Disadvantages of early retirement

Although early retirement can be a useful short-term solution to a need to reduce staffing levels, there are costs associated with this policy. Two out of three respondents in the first IMS survey, although expressing satisfaction with early retirement as a tool for reducing staffing, had doubts about its cost-effectiveness and the long-term implications of pursuing such a policy (IMS 1983). A number of reasons can be cited for these concerns. First, employers operating their own early retirement schemes, may find that they unexpectedly lose more key staff than anticipated. This may be because the scheme is too attractive and/or because access to it is too open. Second, early retirement schemes may prove a more expensive option than originally envisaged by organizations. This may be the result of firms under-estimating the attractiveness of the package on offer; additionally they may fail to put a time limit on the availability of the scheme or realistic budget figure on the overall cost.

A third disadvantage of early retirement, identified by employers as a problem that might occur in the long term, concerns the distortion of the age composition of the work-force if early retirement continued. Early retirement might produce 'humped' age structures which would damage both career prospects and employee motivation.

The disadvantages of JRS for employers were very different. They were less likely to lose skilled staff, and they did not have to bear the cost of early retirement themselves. Moreover, they were probably able to maintain a more balanced age structure in their work-force by replacing older workers. Nevertheless, about 60 per cent of employers perceived some disadvantages associated with JRS (Bushell 1984). The principal disadvantages quoted were the loss of productive employees, the administrative inconvenience, the problem of being restricted to recruitment from job centres and employment offices, and the need to train replacements with the associated costs (Bushell 1984).

The impact of early retirement on unemployment

An important question to consider is the macroeconomic effects of early retirement policies. In doing this we have to consider three main problems. First, the difficulty of distinguishing the effect of early retirement policies from the impact of other policies designed to reduce unemployment; second, estimating how many people might have retired early in the absence of early retirement options; third, calculating how many jobs might have been filled, and under what conditions and for what period of time.

One of the most obvious ways in which early retirement can exert a favourable effect on the unemployment rate of those close to retirement age is when older workers who are already out of work are simply redefined as early retirees and excluded from the official unemployment figures. The extension of the long-term rate of supplementary benefit to long-term unemployed men aged 60–64 in 1981, and to all unemployed men in this age group in 1983, had a significant impact on the official unemployment figures. This effect has generally been accepted as being some 200,000 by the end of October 1983.

A second way in which early retirement can have an effect on unemployment is when it is likely that if an employer had not used early retirement an individual would have been made unemployed. In particular, early retirement can serve to protect the jobs of younger workers when there is a need to reduce manpower. Again it is important to bear in mind the distinction between the JRS scheme and other forms of early retirement. JRS probably did little to protect either older or younger workers in employment from unemployment, because early retirement in these firms was not primarily motivated by a need to reduce staffing levels. However, the JRS did enable these firms to reduce their salary costs and restructure their work-force. Without these changes it is possible that some redundancies might have been necessary.

In France some calculations have been made which suggest that early retirement schemes with a replacement condition such as JRS can have the effect of protecting jobs as well as creating jobs. It is estimated, for example, that the French 'Solidarity Contracts' scheme which operated between 1982 and 1984 on a much larger scale than JRS had the effect of preventing 10,000 redundancies (Lacroix and Guergoat 1984).

In the case of company early retirement plans there is little doubt that many more redundancies would have been declared without early retirement. As noted above, most firms used early retirement primarily in order to reduce manpower. It also seems reasonable to assume that if other means of reducing staffing levels had been adopted, such as the traditional last-in-first-out principle, many more younger workers would have lost their jobs. There may also have been even more redundancies among manual workers of all ages if early retirement schemes, which often were only available to non-manual workers, had not been introduced.

Did early retirement create jobs?

It should be stated at the outset that early retirement can at most maintain labour supply when early retirees are replaced but it does not lead to an increase in labour supply. Therefore, early retirement does not create more jobs in the economy as a whole. As we noted earlier in the chapter, the main reason why employers use early retirement in firms that have developed their own schemes is in order to reduce manpower. It is therefore not surprising that few employers replaced early retirees. Indeed, given that company early retirement is so expensive if used on any large scale, the only way employers can afford to use it, is by securing a very high level of non-replacement (less than 10 per cent) (IMS 1983).

In France in a larger survey of enterprises using early retirement, a similar picture emerges. In 1981 a survey of 2,750 enterprises in the private sector with ten or more employees, employing in total 300,000 people found that only 35 per cent of posts were filled by the hiring of individuals from outside the firm (Ragot 1985). However, even where new people are recruited an employer may well recruit people who already have paid work; hence there is no direct effect on unemployment. Because of this, a number of countries have sought to maximize the job-creation effect of early retirement by imposing a replacement condition which stipulates that employers must recruit those without jobs. Such schemes, which are usually temporary in duration, have been tried in recent years in Austria, Spain, Finland, France, Belgium, Germany and the UK (Laczko 1986). Among these schemes, the JRS appears to have been among the most efficient in terms of reducing unemployment, although less so among young people. A comparison of the effect on unemployment of these schemes in Britain and France has been made (Casey 1985). The impact of early retirement schemes on unemployment is estimated by comparing 'unemployment reduction coefficient figures'. This figure provides a measure of the degree to which early retirement has reduced registered unemployment. It is based on a calculation of the size of the scheme and the extent to which early retirement reduces registered unemployment. It includes various estimates, such as the degree to which early retirees would have retired anyway, under other early retirement options, the fact that some redundancies may have been prevented, the fact that new recruits do not in all instances have to be registered as unemployed etc. The figures presented below refer to separate calculations, made using somewhat different assumptions in Britain and France (for further details, see Casey 1985).

The 'effectiveness coefficient' of the French scheme 'Contrats de

Solidarité, Pre-Retraite Démission' according to various research studies was between 0.5 and 0.65 (Lacroix and Guergoat 1984). On this basis the figure for the total number of unemployed people in France at the end of 1983 (2.23 million) was estimated to be between 89,000 and 116,000 lower than could have been expected in the absence of early retirement. The impact of the much smaller JRS scheme on unemployment was of a similar magnitude. In March 1984 at the peak of JRS coverage, a coefficient of 0.93 was calculated, implying a reduction of 88,000 in registered unemployment, at a time when total registered unemployment stood at 3.14 million. However, given that JRS was much smaller than the French scheme – at its peak JRS recipients numbered 95,000, compared to 178,000 under the French scheme – these figures suggest that JRS may have been more efficient in reducing unemployment in relation to its size (Casey 1985).

The explanation for this seems to be that the labour market authorities in Britain were over the years better able to ensure that persons taking early retirement were replaced. It has to be pointed out that the British scheme began in 1977 (finally ending in 1988) and the French in 1982, thus the British labour market authorities have had more time to operate a job replacement condition. In the first years of the British scheme replacement was much lower. Data supplied from the labour market authorities referring to end of March 1980 suggests an unemployment coefficient of 0.73 as having obtained at that time. The replacement condition was more strongly enforced in later years. British employers were required to provide written evidence of the replacement having occurred, while previously it had been sufficient for employers to agree to endeavour to replace the retiree (Bushell 1984: 20). By contrast in France, French employers were given greater flexibility when fulfilling the replacement condition. Although those replacing retirees had to be recruited from outside the enterprise, recruitment did not have to constitute a direct or even an indirect replacement (Casey 1985). However, JRS seems to have performed less well than some other schemes in creating jobs for unemployed young people. In the case of Belgium's early retirement scheme (the Pre-Pension Légale), for example, all people replacing early retirees were under the age of 30 as the replacement condition stipulated that replacements must be made among this age group. In France, nearly three-quarters of those replacing older workers under the solidarity contracts scheme were under the age of 26 (Ragot 1985: 64). But in Britain only 41 per cent of replacement workers were under the age of 26 over the period 1982–3 (Bushell 1984). One explanation could be that in Belgium and France employers were not required, as in Britain, to employ a 'replacement worker' on an unlimited contract of employment. Instead appointments needed to be made only for a period of at least twelve months (France) or six months (Belgium). Another factor could be that it was more difficult in the UK to find direct replacements for older workers among younger workers.

To sum up, early retirement has had the effect of taking a sizeable proportion of unemployed older workers out of the official unemployment figures. It has also had the effect of protecting a large number of younger workers from unemployment, albeit at the expense of older workers withdrawing from the labour force. However, early retirement has not created substantial opportunities for unemployed people. First, because under most company schemes the early retired are not replaced, and even when they are replaced there is no requirement to give priority to the employment of the unemployed. Second, in the case of Britain, JRS was only a modest early retirement scheme. Although it was efficient, a relatively small number of jobs were created for unemployed people and especially the young unemployed, in relation to the level of unemployment in Britain during the period in which it was in operation.

Conclusion: early exit in the 1990s

Between 1987 and 1995 the number of 16–24-year-olds in the labour force is projected to fall by 1.2 million, a decline of one-fifth – with a decline of 23 per cent in the 16–19-year-old age group. This means that many employers will be looking to find alternative sources of labour, given a situation in which the decline in the number of younger workers will continue throughout the 1990s. Yet the evidence at present is that employers are unlikely to reverse policies which (as we discussed in Chapter 4) have discriminated heavily against older workers (see also National Economic Development Office 1989). Projections for activity rates up to the year 2000 suggest further declines for men over 60, with little change for men and women aged 55–59.

Recent research with respect to Germany suggests that in the 1990s there may be a growing conflict between the social policy of the firm and the social policy of the state in regard to early retirement (Jacobs and Rein 1988). The state wants to reverse the current trend towards early retirement because it is expensive, particularly when the population is ageing and the number of young people entering the work-force is falling. However, employers may wish to pursue early retirement policies because this will enable them to restructure their work-force more effectively. Early retirement also gives them a socially acceptable instrument for reducing their workforce should the need arise. Jacobs, Kohli and Rein (1987) argue that although some firms will reverse the trend towards early retirement this is unlikely to be the case for the economy as a whole. They found that even expanding industries had substantially reduced their older work-force in recent years, albeit at a lower rate than in declining industries. They conclude therefore that

> early retirement is a general trend rather than an industry-specific trend. It takes place almost everywhere – in growing and declining industries – although not to the same degree. The similarities of this trend are more important than the variations.
>
> (Jacobs *et al*. 1987: 30)

This scenario is also broadly applicable to Britain, although there are some important differences. The state in Britain has played a less active role in promoting early retirement than in Germany, while employers in the UK have played a much more active part in developing private early retirement options than German employers.

Although use of early retirement in Britain is primarily motivated by the need to reduce staffing, there is also evidence that early retirement helps many firms to alter the skill-mix of their personnel and perhaps also reduce salary costs. Early retirement is therefore not merely a cyclical phenomenon. Many firms may wish to continue to use early retirement even if unemployment falls further, and indeed they may face pressure from their employees to do so. It seems likely that the extensive use of early retirement in many firms in recent years has lead to an expectation among employees that they too will be offered early retirement. Early retirement seems to have changed employee perceptions particularly among white-collar staff, to the extent that many now expect a shorter working life and at least some control over the point at which they retire (McGoldrick 1983). Fewer workers now plan to remain at work until state pension age and many, particularly at management level, take advantage of Additional Voluntary Contribution options within their pension schemes to allow them to retire early on a non-reduced pension (Institute of Manpower Studies 1987). To conclude, early retirement practices may have become so established in some of Britain's larger enterprises that they will become difficult to reverse in the future. All of this has radical implications in the context of an ageing work-force, one which is set to diminish in size during the first quarter of the twenty-first century. To what extent are we likely to see attempts by the state to encourage older workers to delay their retirement (as was the case in a similar period of labour shortage in the 1950s)? Will there be tensions between generations when pension promises made when the ratio of workers to pensioners was high are perceived as difficult to deliver (Ermisch 1990; Johnson *et al*. 1989)? Questions such as these indicate that we must consider the politics of early exit in the post-war period, and particularly within the context of future demographic change. It is this area that we shall discuss in Chapter 7.

7

The politics of
early exit

Introduction

We have assessed the development of early retirement in the UK during the 1970s and 1980s. A theme pursued in different parts of the book has been that early exit took place in the absence of action by the state to finance secure routes out of the labour force. Instead, negotiating and financing early exit was left to organizations and individuals, with the state mainly providing encouragement within a context of economic recession and high unemployment. But this lack of involvement by the state as regards financing early retirement itself reflects considerable uncertainty about the way forward in respect of developing a policy for retirement. What develops in this period is, on the one hand, recognition by government that new policies in relation to the timing of retirement are needed; that, in particular, the conventional retirement ages of 60 and 65 should be made more flexible, and that new attitudes to work and leisure are creating the climate for a different approach. On the other hand, how to move forward given the potential costs of lowering the retirement age is seen as a major obstacle to reform.

In the absence of any clear lead from government there was, none the less, an intense debate throughout this period reviewing the case for introducing greater flexibility into the retirement system. The aim of this chapter is to examine the positions taken on flexible retirement by different political actors, focusing, in particular, on government, the trade unions, business organizations and pressure groups. Our argument will be that the debate around early exit has functioned at two levels. On the one hand, the majority of political actors have supported the case for a flexible system of retirement – with the possibility of individuals working beyond normal retirement age as well as retiring before it. On the other hand, within the context of high levels of unemployment, there has been a tendency to accelerate the pace of early exit, through, for example, the modification of pension schemes, the use of redundancy payments and the development of special programmes such as the job release scheme (JRS).

In fact, developments in the 1980s confirm the validity of the view that the state has used older workers as a reserve army of labour to be ejected or encouraged to stay at work, according to perceptions of demographic change and the likely supply of younger workers (Phillipson 1982). Although this has been criticized as a 'conspiratorial interpretation of the process of early retirement' (Johnson *et al.*1989: 12), it would appear to have strong empirical support from the experience of older workers over the last ten years. The failure to resolve the question of flexibility itself reflects limited interest in moving from a policy which has proved flexible for those concerned with losing manpower in periods of crisis. Underpinning this are more recent anxieties about the long-term cost of demographic change and the willingness of the younger generation to finance the pensions of the old (Ermisch 1990). To what extent these concerns will continue to frustrate progress on the debate about flexibility is a subject we shall review in the latter part of this chapter. First, however, we shall explore the debate during the 1970s and 1980s concerning the age of retirement.

Perspectives on retirement

It was suggested above that there has been considerable uncertainty about how to implement reform on the question of retirement ages for men and women. Part of this uncertainty must be attributed to wider concerns about people's ability to cope with the loss of work. As King and Stearns write:

> A cultural history of gerontological literature would note that its authors are often work enthusiasts themselves who find it difficult to imagine a satisfactory life divorced from employment. This is not to say that their judgement is wrong . . . and in individual cases empirical results on the problems posed by retirement have been impressive. There is a tendency, however, to assume a capacity for continued work that is not in turn empirically tested, rather reversing, but not necessarily improving upon, the exaggerated sense of elderly decay that dominated the literature of the nineteenth century.
>
> (King and Stearns 1981: 595)

This cultural pessimism about retirement probably had two effects on the debate over pension ages. On the part of government, there were two conflicting positions in this period. In the first half of the 1970s the argument tended to be that no change at all was probably the best option; that any adjustment in the retirement age could have adverse social effects in terms of adjustment to the loss of work (see for example DHSS 1976). In the 1980s this position was (as we shall see) relaxed somewhat, with the argument for a 'decade of retirement' being developed, albeit with the cost implications still a matter of concern (see p. 102). On the part of other agencies, there was a commitment to the idea of flexible retirement, this to allow more older workers to continue working past 60 or 65, in line with their own preferences. Perspectives on retirement were, of course, to undergo radical change in the light of the trends discussed in this book. But the debate on retirement ages had, by the 1980s developed its own momentum, with most organizations reaffirming their belief in the virtues of a flexible approach.

Changing the age of retirement

The case for flexible retirement has been widely discussed in the post-war period. The arguments in its favour received extensive coverage in Michel Fogarty's (1975) important study: *40 to 60: How We Waste the Middle Aged*. A major concern of Fogarty's study was that we were wasting the skills of the mature adult, whether in the context of work, education or voluntary activity in the community. In relation to work, while recognizing the problems involved, he made a detailed case for adopting a flexible approach to retirement age. Fogarty summarized the dilemmas, together with his own solution, in the following way:

> Flexible time and longer or more varied vacations or sabbaticals can help to give people the control of their own time which they need later in life. It remains, however, to reconcile the need for flexibility in retirement with what is practicable in terms of the other commitments of the community. Early retirement involves either a heavy financial charge on the active population or a substantial cut in the pensioner's annual entitlement, whose effect will be felt most at the time when he finally gives up earnings at age seventy onwards. It may also mean some loss to the national income through a reduction in the work force, though this can be offset if more pensioners are encouraged to continue in part-time work. . . . One possible solution might be to spread formal retiring ages over the years from, say, 62 to 70,

but to pay pensions (except in the case of the disabled) at only half rate between these ages.

(Fogarty 1975: 234)

A variation on these arguments was developed two years later by Pilch and Carroll (1977), where they put forward a modified version of the Swedish model of partial retirement. They proposed a transition to a retirement decade of 60 to 70 for men and women. The 'standard' pension age for both would be 65. Between ages 60 and 65 both men and women would be entitled to draw the basic social security pension at half rate, or alternatively a tax-free cash bonus, payable at 65 or later retirement, of 30 per cent of basic pension for each year by which they deferred drawing a pension up to 65.

The attractions of a flexible retirement age were extensively discussed in many of the submissions to the House of Commons Social Services Committee (1982) inquiry into the age of retirement. Here we find a virtual consensus from many of the organizations and individuals called to give evidence, that a flexible system was both a realistic and a desirable goal of social policy. The Confederation of British Industry (CBI) argued that there should 'as a matter of urgency' be flexibility for people to retire early on a reduced pension. At the same time, increased pensions should also be given to those who defer 'retirement' thus creating a 'valuable incentive to persuade key workers to continue in employment' (House of Commons 1982: 275).

Age Concern, one of the major voluntary organizations campaigning on behalf of older people, put forward a proposal that

A flexible retirement system should be introduced with legislation to ensure that there is no compulsory retirement, on age related grounds, before the age of 70. Any minimum pension age should not, in effect, become a compulsory retirement age and legislation would be essential if the minimum pension age is lowered.

(House of Commons 1982: 241)

At the same time, it would be misleading to suggest that there was total consensus, in the submissions to the House of Commons Committee, regarding the adoption of a flexible retirement. The two major exceptions were the trade unions and pressure groups representing working class pensioners. For these organizations, the main demand was for a common retirement age of 60 years coupled with a substantial increase in the state pension. Three factors influenced their perspective: first, the impact of mass unemployment; second, the reduced life expectancy of working-class men and women; third, the reliance by manual workers on the state retirement pension.

In terms of the employment issue, there has been a tendency to see a common age at 60 as a means of creating job opportunities for the young. As Ray Buckton put it, in presenting the TUC's submission to the House of Commons Social Services Committee:

> Now we have millions of people who are not working, and we are having to pay them to sit at home doing nothing at the present time. Perhaps we could shift that to people over sixty, and let them retire gracefully with an adequate pension, thereby letting these younger people come into industry and start producing the wealth that we are looking for.
>
> (House of Commons 1982: 148)

This view was echoed by evidence to the House of Commons Committee from the National Pensioners' Convention Steering Committee, a group closely linked to the trades union movement. They argued that

> Earlier retirement is desirable to provide more job opportunities, to achieve equality between men and women and, particularly, to permit people who have given perhaps forty years services to the British economy to enjoy their last years of life in relative ease. . . . Our Declaration of Intent spells out that people should as of right be eligible for an adequate retirement pension on ceasing work, at any time of their choice after the age of 60 years, without being subject to an earnings rule. In our view an 'adequate' income is a pension level of not less than half average gross earnings, for a married couple, not less than one-third of average gross earnings for a single person, uprated at six-monthly intervals. We would oppose any general move to early retirement which does not guarantee a proper income to the pensioner.
>
> (House of Commons 1982: 373)

Earlier retirement is also seen to be justified because of the harsh working environment for those in manual occupations. The view of the General and Municipal Workers' Union (GMWU), is representative of this argument:

> The GMWU's policy on Pensions and Retirement is influenced by the experience of our members. Thousands of GMWU members work in dangerous and hazardous jobs, for example as gypsum miners, in the chemical industry, and with asbestos. Many do not survive to collect their pension at 65. Among our thermal insulation engineering members, for example, the

average age of death from occupational causes is 54. Thermal insulation engineering workers constitute half per cent of our membership but by 1980 accounted for 30 per cent of claims for union's occupational death benefit. About 50 per cent of our thermal insulation engineering membership directly exposed to asbestos say for 20 years can expect to die prematurely from industrial disease. The hazardous nature of many occupations is one of the principal motivations for the repeated and urgent call for progress towards reduction of the retirement age for men.

(House of Commons 1982: 337)

Despite such arguments, the trade union case for retirement at 60 has been firmly rejected by successive governments; on the other hand, there has been little progress towards flexible retirement. Flexibility (in terms of both higher and lower retirement ages) may have been popular as a statement of intent and goodwill to older workers; as a realistic policy, in a period of high unemployment, it has been seen as having little to commend it. The key political actor here has been governments, with both Labour and Conservative administrations in the 1970s and 1980s encouraging discussions on the viability of flexible retirement, while carefully avoiding any firm commitment regarding implementation.

State policies towards retirement age

For governments, the problem has been that neither flexibility nor a common retirement age (at 60 or 63 years) on a full state pension, have been viewed as realistic in a context of budgetary constraints and competing social priorities. Thus creating greater flexibility in the age of retirement is seen as administratively complex as well as entailing a substantial financial cost to industry and the taxpayer. A common retirement age of 60 or 63 years has been viewed as even more expensive and likely to place an unacceptable burden on economic resources.

At the same time, Labour and Conservative governments have shared the view that flexibility is at least preferable to equalizing the age of retirement and they have recognized, in addition, the political support behind such a change in policy. While accepting the case for flexibility, however, uncertainty has been expressed about the process of implementation. The Labour government's discussion paper, *A Happier Old Age* (DHSS 1978), reviewed the various arguments regarding a common and a flexible retirement age, and invited the general public to join the debate. The White Paper *Growing Older* (DHSS 1981b), a product of the first Thatcher administration, identified the issues relating to a flexible retirement age between 60 and 70:

> At whatever 'normal' point was chosen, men and women would have the choice of taking their full pension and continuing to work full-time or part-time with no earnings rule; deferring their pension to earn a higher one when they wished to retire or of giving work up altogether. Men and women who wish to retire before that age could do so on a reduced pension.
>
> (DHSS 1981b: 18)

The White Paper concluded that while spending constraints prevented short-term considerations of such a proposal, it should be kept in view as a 'long-term objective'. However, the proposals for the reform of social security, which emerged in the second Thatcher government, still held back from taking the debate any further. Indeed, after rehearsing the now familiar arguments, the government returned to a position similar to that of the Labour government in 1978:

> . . . combining a common pension age with effective and worthwhile provision for flexible retirement, has attractions as a long-term aid and seems to offer the best prospect of an acceptable solution. Current constraints on spending preclude early changes. Nevertheless, the Government intends to keep such an arrangement in view as a long-term objective.
>
> (DHSS 1981b: 18)

The issue of costs was in fact to continue to frustrate progress in moving to a common retirement age. The House of Commons Select Committee on Social Services (1982) were to recommend a common retirement age of 63. The government, however, took the view that even this compromise would, at £500 million per year, be too expensive. The Green Paper on the *Reform of Social Security* (DHSS 1985) renewed the idea of a 'decade of retirement', only to state that there would still have to be some restrictions on how this operated, namely that 'those wishing to retire early and receive an abated national insurance pension would have to demonstrate that they had sufficient private provision to ensure that they would not be dependent on income-related state support to supplement the abated pension' (DHSS 1985a: 26–7).

The attractions of the retirement decade have also been reaffirmed by the Labour Party. According to their policy review document: 'Labour's objective is to make the period from 60 and 70 a decade of flexibility in which both men and women are entitled to retire on full pension or to continue in work without discrimination on the grounds of age' (cited in Schuller and Walker 1990: 13).

The new politics of retirement: workers versus pensioners?

Despite the idea of flexibility being supported on both the Right and the Left of the political spectrum, in reality the decade of the 1980s made limited progress towards this policy. Instead, as we have seen, a range of measures emerged to promote early exit – particularly for those on low incomes, in poor health and/or in contracting industries. The phenomenon of early exit thus emerged within the context of political inertia over flexible retirement and opposition to the equalization of retirement ages at 60 or 63. In comparison to the numerous political groups demanding action on unemployment, the forces pressing for a coherent policy on retirement were neither as united nor as unambiguous in their demands. Moreover, by the late 1980s another set of concerns had surfaced in relation to the issue of retirement: namely, were the promises of early retirement or even retirement at 60/65 really sustainable given the increased costs of pensions and the sharp decline (especially in the twenty-first century) in the ratio of workers to pensioners? This debate was foreshadowed by a number of discussions in Britain and the USA in the early 1980s (Fogarty 1982; Preston 1984; DHSS 1985) but was to emerge with renewed vigour in the late 1980s and early 1990s, in particular with the publication of a collection of readings edited by Johnson, Conrad and Thompson (1989), entitled *Workers versus Pensioners: Intergenerational Justice in an Ageing World*.

In Britain the agenda for this debate was set by the first Thatcher administration, where concern was expressed in keynote speeches by ministers, that workers were reassessing how much of their taxes should go towards supporting pensions for retired people. Older people were depicted as playing 'havoc with the Exchequer's budget' (*Sunday Times*, 28 August 1983), undermining attempts to restrict public expenditure and to reduce the overall level of taxation. The possibility of intergenerational conflict over resources was subsequently taken up by academics and political commentators, with suggestions that older people had created a comprehensive welfare state for themselves while reducing equivalent resources for younger people (Johnson *et al.* 1989).

The argument about the emerging conflict between workers and pensioners was set out in some detail by David Thompson (1989) in a paper entitled 'The welfare state and generational conflict: winners and losers'. The 'winners', according to Thompson, were older people who had been able to 'capture' the welfare state and design it in a way which ensured that their own needs are adequately met. Conversely the 'losers' were younger people who, asked to pay an increasingly larger share of their income to support older people, are likely to find that there is very little left for themselves when they reach retirement age. At the same time, it is argued that benefits for older people continue to expand, the growth in the income of the old outstripping younger people with families. Using the example of New Zealand (data from which were used to speculate about trends in Europe and the USA), Thompson found that the single-income young family of two children had 20 per cent less real purchasing power than it did in 1960; conversely the elderly household had 100 per cent more.

It is also suggested that younger people are themselves becoming more aware of the extent to which they are being denied resources and are working for a future which cannot be properly financed. According to Thompson, 'The young, whatever their income levels, have been learning some important lessons about their welfare state in the 1970s and 1980s – that it does not deliver, and that it has no intention of giving them what older citizens once enjoyed' (Thompson 1989: 44). As a consequence, it is argued that younger people may rebel from a welfare contract which seems to work against their interests and will support the policies of right-wing governments in respect of efforts to restructure the welfare state. The outcome of this will be increasing conflict between generations which, it is argued, 'may affect not just the relative welfare of the old and the young, but [may] also threaten the very existence of state welfare systems' (Johnson et al. 1989: 7).

In France, Xavier Gaullier (1988a) has expressed a similar view, suggesting that demographic and retirement trends are a threat to social cohesion.

We are already witnessing the emergence of conflicts between the generations which are bound to get worse in years to come. Will the working part of the population accept to pay for the retirement pensions of those not working, who will become increasingly numerous and increasingly capable of working? Will those not working, excluded from the labour market, accept a progressive diminution of the level of their retirement or early retirement benefits? Will young and older workers come more and more into conflict with one another in competing for jobs and careers? Alongside the conflicts between social classes and

between the sexes, conflicts between the generations may well
become more and more pronounced in the decades ahead.

(Gaullier 1988a: 2–3)

Supporting retirement: an alternative view

The workers versus pensioners thesis contains a number of propo-
sitions relating to the future viability of the welfare state and the
willingness of younger people to sustain high levels of public
expenditure (Phillipson 1991). In this book, however, we shall
concentrate on the arguments relating to the alleged 'problems'
created by the growth in the non-productive sector of the population,
that is the increase in the number of retired people relative to that of
people of working age. Here we should note at the outset the timeless
nature both of the arguments and the language used to describe older
people. Nearly forty years separate the following observations, both
making roughly the same point about the 'burden' of old age:

> The growing increase in the proportion of older persons in the
> population will inevitably mean an increase in the amount of
> current production required for their maintenance. The cost
> must not be recognised only in terms of family help towards their
> support or of the proportion of the pension that comes from
> public funds, but in terms of their contribution to the com-
> munity's production and services.
>
> (Phillips Report 1954: 11)

> An inevitable corollary of this reduction in the number of years
> spent in employment is an increase in the length of life spent
> dependent on the effort and output of that section of the
> population currently engaged in productive work. . . .Whether
> the retired population is supported from its own savings or from
> state pension and welfare payments does not affect the general
> proposition that the present consumption of the aged (and
> children) is provided for by the current output of productive
> workers.
>
> (Johnson et al. 1989: 4)

What is interesting about these statements is that they are operating in
very similar contexts: first, a perception that the problem of poverty
among older people is now confined to a minority; second, an
associated view that the incomes of retired people are now 'on a par
with [those] of non-aged persons' (Thompson 1989: 52); third, an
experience of labour shortages which is seen to undermine the

legitimacy of retirement. Such historical consistencies do not invalidate views about the economic problems generated by population change; they do suggest, however, that we are dealing with a question not simply of political economy but also an ideological assessment of older people in general and retirement in particular (Phillipson and Walker 1987).

Productivity in an ageing world

Let us, though, try and make some assessment of the long-term impact of demographic trends. In particular, will the ageing of our population so adversely affect the relative size of the labour force and/or its productivity as to reduce both economic growth and improvements in the standard of living? If we look at the situation in Britain between 1985 and 2015 we actually see only a slight change in the ratio of National Insurance contributors to pensioners (see Table 7.1). There is then a sharper downturn in the ratio between 2015 and 2035. After that the indications are for a levelling off with a gradual growth in the labour force relative to the younger and retired population. There is no question, however, that significant trends can be discerned in respect of the overall ratio of people of working age (15–64) to those aged 65 and over. These are set out in Table 7.2 for a selected group of European countries. Again, the figures do show considerable decreases in the worker–pensioner ratio during the first three decades of the twenty-first century. But two immediate observations might be made about both these figures and those in Table 7.1. First, there is no radical change in the ratio for some twenty years, a point which reminds us that we are attempting to make the

Table 7.1 Demographic factors affecting pensions

Year	Pensioners (millions)	National Insurance contributors (millions)	Ratio of National Insurance contributors to pensioners
1985	9.3	21.8	2.3
1995	9.8	21.9	2.2
2005	10.0	22.2	2.2
2015	11.1	22.4	2.0
2025	12.3	21.9	1.8
2035	13.2	21.8	1.6

Source: DHSS 1985a: vol. 2: 4

Table 7.2   Ratio of people aged 15–64 to people aged 65 and over (selected countries)

	1960	1980	2000	2025	Ratio 1980/ 1960	Ratio 2025/ 2000
Austria	5.46	4.17	4.27	2.87	0.764	0.672
Belgium	5.41	4.57	4.05	2.95	0.845	0.729
Finland	8.70	5.65	4.74	2.77	0.649	0.584
France	5.32	4.57	4.24	3.01	0.859	0.711
Greece	7.94	4.88	3.89	3.01	0.615	0.774
Italy	7.04	4.90	4.02	2.90	0.696	0.722
Luxembourg	6.25	5.00	4.33	2.66	0.800	0.614
Netherlands	6.76	5.75	4.85	2.65	0.851	0.545
Norway	5.68	4.27	4.17	3.00	0.752	0.721
Spain	7.81	5.88	4.39	3.38	0.753	0.770
Sweden	5.52	3.94	3.72	2.60	0.714	0.701
United Kingdom	5.56	4.26	4.24	3.12	0.766	0.735

Source: Adapted from Ermisch 1990: 45, Table 6

kind of long-range forecasts which can be made only with consider-able restraint: rather more, in fact, than has been characteristic of the debate in this area.

Second, the figures in Table 7.2 confirm that virtually all in-dustrialized economies have already assimilated (with varying degrees of success) downward changes in worker pensioner ratios. Indeed, the shift between 1960 and 1980 was for many countries of a similar magnitude to that predicted for the turn of the century. Clearly though, the secular trend is of considerable significance and raises many important issues. Will this development lead to greater conflict over the distribution of resources, between a relatively small labour force confronting a large pensioner population? Are we likely to see cuts in pensions as an alternative to unacceptably high levels of contribution rates paid by the working population?

In fact, there may be a number of reasons for questioning whether changes in the ratio of workers to pensioners will inevitably lead to conflict. First, the impact of a change in the ratio has to be related to overall levels of employment. For example the International Labour Organization (ILO) (1989) has argued that the UK will be able to cushion the effect of an ageing population by continuing to cut levels of unemployment. Thus if unemployment remained at the level it was in 1985, the ratio of people over 60 to those aged 20–65 would increase 23.2 per cent by 2025. If, on the other hand, unemployment was eradicated, this dependency ratio would actually fall by 16.7 per cent (ILO 1989; see also Falkingham 1989).

Second, the argument that population ageing will have a damaging effect on productivity needs to be examined with caution. In a detailed assessment of this issue in the context of the American economy, Palmer and Gould (1986) put forward some predictions about the impact of demographic change on per capita economic growth. They use four main variables: labour force to population growth; capital per worker; labour quality and efficiency; technological change. They note a number of positive features about demographic change which might also be transposed to other capitalist economies: that (as observed on p. 106) dependency ratios will not substantially 'deteriorate' until we are into the second decade of the twenty-first century; that during this period (and for a variety of reasons) there will be a greater concentration of capital per worker and therefore, all things being equal, more output per worker; that the general ageing of the labour force over a broad range of occupations will increase its overall productivity; that there will be improved prospects for increasing the quantity and quality of general education and training per worker. Palmer and Gould conclude that even on the basis of somewhat pessimistic estimates about future population growth, '[such changes] should no more inhibit rising standards of living over the fifty years than it has in the past' (Palmer and Gould 1986: 373). In short, apocalyptic views about too many elderly people causing a threat to the viability of western economies must, for the moment, be suspended.

At the same time, we might put forward another type of argument, namely that the pessimism from Thompson and his colleagues is partly due to somewhat restricted notions of productivity. Neugarten and Neugarten (1986) make the valuable point

> that the aging society will need a broader definition of productivity than the one that is current today, a definition that goes beyond participation in the labour force and extends to non-paid roles. These would include not only those that are attached to formally organised voluntary associations, but also to services that individuals provide to family members both inside and outside the household, services to neighbours and friends, and self-care activities. The need is to seek out and nurture the potential for social productivity, in this broad sense, wherever it is to be found – not only among the young-old, but among younger people as well.
>
> (Neugarten and Neugarten 1986: 48)

Third, the extent to which population change will represent a burden
will also depend on future prospects for economic growth (itself
linked to changes in productivity). In a report published by the
Institute for Fiscal Studies, Fry *et al.* (1990) have examined the
average tax rate required to finance the flat rate pension scheme under
alternative scenarios for real wage growth and unemployment levels.
They conclude that

> Even on the modest assumption about the rate of growth, the
> level of Gross Domestic Product (GDP) available to finance
> specific services for the elderly will be substantially higher in
> 2030 than now; an annual growth rate of 2% would more than
> double the level of GDP over the whole period. In the context of
> economic growth of this sort, the public expenditure costs of
> health and social services provision for 33% more over 65s by the
> year 2030 appear easily affordable, if the cost per pensioner stays
> at current levels.
>
> (Fry *et al.* 1990: 27)

The caveat at the end is important: first, because the real cost of
public services is, as the authors point out, likely to rise over the
longer term; second, the current living standards of the majority of
pensioners (particularly women) urgently needs to be raised: achieving this will inevitably increase costs per pensioner over the next few
decades.

These qualifications apart, we would also make two general points
in criticism of the worker versus pensioner thesis. First, we need to
start questioning many of the assumptions made in extrapolations
from changes in dependency ratios. For example it is assumed that
aged dependants represent a greater per capita cost than young
dependants. However, some economists have questioned the ad-
equacy of current information on the relative 'costs' of young and old
people. Schulz (1980) cites a West German study which found that
the total cost of rearing a child to 20 is one-quarter to one-third than is
needed to support a 60-year-old for the rest of his or her life.

Second, and more importantly, we perhaps need to start revising
the traditional way in which dependency ratios are calculated.
Typically, either segmental ratios are used (comparing the population
65 and over with that aged 18–64) or labour force dependency ratios
(comparing the numbers of workers to non-workers). But a more
satisfactory approach may be to take a wider definition of productivity
and include within the productive age group people aged 65–74. This
might be justified on the basis of the contributions made by this group
to the maintenance of family and community life (as illustrated on

p. 108) as well as to the direct contribution of a minority to the economy (in various forms of part-time and self-employment). Using this approach, and given that the majority of people in this age group can live independently in the community, we are likely to produce more optimistic scenarios of future demographic trends than traditional approaches would suggest (see Friedmann and Adamchak 1983 for a discussion along these lines).

Third, it might be observed that in making predictions into the twenty-first century, it is important to recognize wider political, cultural and social transformations which might modify the changes under discussion. For example the argument in the study by Johnson *et al*. (1989) assumes that economies will continue to operate largely within national boundaries. Yet it is barely conceivable, given the pace of change in the European community, that this will be the case. In fact, the possibilities for much more permeable national boundaries and hence labour markets are such that we might envisage the flexible transfer of workers to areas where particular skills are in short supply (something which is already beginning to happen). Such developments will allow us to modify, albeit in a small way, the most pessimistic assumptions about the economic impact of demographic change.

Conclusion

This chapter has reviewed some of the policy arguments relating to the debate over changing the age of retirement. It is clear that a consensus view has emerged that change is necessary, in particular towards the idea of a 'decade of retirement', but that achieving this still raises many economic and political difficulties. Progress on this debate has been further frustrated through the re-emergence of the notion of possible intergenerational conflict over the burden posed by the growth in retirement pensions. We have raised some critical points about this issue. Certainly we would question the view that the future growth of retirement is likely to pose insuperable problems for the economy. What is at issue is the need to develop an effective policy for retirement, one which provides both security for older workers and which encourages their participation in a range of work and non-work activities. It is to this area that we now turn.

8
The future of
retirement

Introduction

This book has reviewed a number of important trends as regards the emergence of early exit and early retirement. The key developments may be listed as follows: first, the rapid increase in the numbers of people leaving work ahead of state retirement age (by the mid-1990s about half of men in the 55–65 age group will be outside paid employment). Second, the ambiguity in terms of social status which affects many in this age group. Thus although the *de facto* normal age at which the majority of men cease to work may no longer be 65, most older men do not consider themselves to be 'retired' until 65. However, we also noted important social class differences in this latter respect, with men in social classes I and II being much more likely to describe themselves as retired in comparison to those from social classes V and VI. Equally striking is the fact that the majority of women do not retire at 60, or at least they do not consider that they have retired. In the LFS study only one-third of women describe themselves as retirees; even at age 74 only 56 per cent of women say that they have retired.

An important argument in this book is that this move away from the conventional retirement age has not been buttressed by a range of social policies to support older workers. As Bosanquet notes: 'the predominant aim has been to reduce unemployment – or rather the unemployment statistics' (Bosanquet 1987: 28). Indeed, in a comparative study of the treatment of older workers, Casey and Bruche suggested that the UK in the 1980s still presented itself as 'an example of a country where the policy for older workers is almost non-existent' (Casey and Bruche 1983). The lack of policy in this area itself reflects (as we saw in Chapter 7) uncertainty about how to move forward on issues relating to the age of retirement. This has been primarily associated with the potential costs associated with any change from the traditional ages. However, the result has been that the costs of early exit have been shifted to the individual retiree. Here there is the potential problem of people who took early retirement in the 1970s and 1980s finding that while the initial years of retirement are tolerable, the later years may bring difficulties arising from dwindling savings, loss of any part-time work, major house repairs, and a reduction in the purchasing value of any occupational pension. These problems are of course underpinned by the declining value of the state retirement pension, the change in the uprating link to prices alone making the 1989 National Insurance retirement pension for a married couple £17.50 per week (or 25 per cent) *less* than what it would have been under the old system.

The paradox of early exit

A major conclusion to be drawn from this study is that while a radical change in the employment position of older workers has emerged, the social consequences of this have yet to be fully acknowledged at the level of central government. There are at least four reasons that can be cited for this: first, the failure to predict or plan for the decline in activity rates; second, the changing composition of the labour market; third, the development of the worker versus pensioner debate; fourth, continuing doubts about the value of retirement as a social institution. On the first point, early exit was in no sense a planned or predicted development. Even up to the mid-1960s, the then Ministry of Labour was projecting that, based on trends up to 1965, economic activity rates for older men and women would remain stable over the period 1966 to 1981 (Ministry of Labour Gazette 1967). The expectation was that economic activity rates for men would continue exactly as they were, at 98 per cent for men aged 50–54, 96 per cent for 55–59 and 90 per cent for 60–64-year-olds. A slight dip, from 38 per cent in 1966 to 30.5 per cent in 1981, was envisaged for those aged 65 and over. For women the rates were seen as holding steady for those not married, at 62 per cent for 55–59-year-olds and 29 per cent for 60–64-year-olds, and increasing for married women, from 39 per cent to 52 per cent and 21 per cent to 26 per cent for the respective age groups. Tom Schuller comments on these figures:

> That the projections were well wide of the mark for the male rates is evident. What is more striking is the assumption made then of constancy in the pattern of labour force participation. The rates for men of all ages up to 65 were seen as straightforwardly

remaining for fifteen years at the level of the first half of the 1960s. Had the projections been accurate, the current generation of men would indeed have been repeating the pattern of their predecessors. To point to the inaccuracy is not to exploit hindsight unfairly; it is simply to underline the difficulty of anticipating changes in the pattern of institutional time. And even if such changes are anticipated, they may not be catered for.

(Schuller 1989: 45)

Clearly, in relation to early exit both these last points by Schuller are of relevance. The lack of planning is one thing. A more fundamental observation, however, is that the state failed, even when the strength of the decline in activity rates was recognized (and, indeed, in part facilitated by governments) to secure high status and financially secure routes out of the labour force. Instead, there were a number of uncoordinated moves by different government departments leading to the creation of early exit work but down routes which were, in the main, poorly financed and of low social status.

Unfortunately the incentives to correct this situation were reduced by a second factor which came into play in the 1980s, namely the perception that the labour market, while not shrinking in the immediate future, was changing its composition, with a steep decline in the number of young people. Employers were now urged to look for alternative sources of labour, including workers aged over 50 (National Economic Development Office 1989). The *Sunday Times* reported that in the 1990s it was likely that 'the elderly will be encouraged to stay in paid employment until they are 70 or even older'. Norman Fowler (the then Secretary of State for Employment) was quoted as saying:

We are challenging the whole concept that retirement ages should get earlier and earlier. It should be left to individuals to decide when to retire. . . . The present 60/65 fixed retirement ages are totally misconceived. . . . There is going to be much greater scope for people to continue in their careers for much longer, and greater value will be placed on their experience than ever before.

(*Sunday Times* 29 January 1989)

Moves to improve the position of the early retired have been further undermined by the worker versus pensioner debate highlighted in Chapter 7. The argument from Paul Johnson and his colleagues was that while early retirement may benefit the retirees and the individual firm or organization, the gains for the working population were less clear. Thus if intergenerational competition for jobs was one of the factors in pushing people out of the labour force (Cowgill 1974), intergenerational conflict over resources was now being cited as a key factor in demanding that they be brought back into employment. Johnson and his colleagues noted the problems for workers in terms of them having to support 'the cost of generous pension arrangements either through increased taxes, increased private contributions, or increased prices for the products of the companies that promote these expensive early retirement policies' (Johnson *et al.* 1989: 11). The authors see a conflict between two public goods – the short-term labour market concern and the long-term pension cost concern. They point to the need to return to a higher level of labour force participation by older workers as in the interest of economies which face the problem of population ageing.

In short, if early exit from work was a largely unforeseen development, its arrival has, in the 1990s, been seen as a short-term expediency but not an arrangement which can be justified over the longer term. But the social consequences have been resisted for at least one other reason: namely the continuing doubts about the value and merits of retirement as social institution. Here we might argue that the ambiguity surrounding 'work-ending' (Schuller 1989) itself feeds into the cultural pessimism about retirement referred to at the beginning of Chapter 7. But early exit has also brought to the surface contradictions in social and individual attitudes to retirement. On the one hand, it is clear that the expectation of early retirement has spread to a substantial segment of the population. A public opinion survey carried out in 1989 found 48 per cent of men and 44 per cent of women thought that they would retire at 55 or less, and 20 per cent of men and 23 per cent of women thought they would retire at 50 or less (ICM/*Sunday Correspondent* 31 December 1989). Moreover, the sociological literature on retirement gives ground for suggesting that there is a secular trend towards more positive retirement attitudes. Markides and Cooper (1987) have gone as far to argue that 'No longer can we keep on writing that the transition to retirement is particularly difficult because of lack of appropriate socialisation to the retired role. For better or for worse more and more people are retiring and more of them are having fun being retired' (Markides and Cooper 1987: 7; see also Phillipson 1987; 1990a). But it was precisely this situation that came to be questioned within the context of assertions about the possibility of intergenerational conflict. Here we had the image of a hedonistic welfare generation, enjoying resources which could no longer be guaranteed for young adults. The paradox of early exit is thus that its arrival has run in parallel with doubts as to both its legitimacy and viability within a changing economic and demographic world. This is, of course, an undesirable situation – from all points of view. In Britain in the 1990s, a majority of men are now permanently outside the labour force before state retirement age, but with the legitimacy of their position now under attack. However, we would question whether simply posing the possibility of intergenerational conflict and/or of urging for a return to work by the old, are adequate responses to the challenges before us. We would argue that the worker versus pensioner debate has been unhelpful because it has obstructed constructive thinking about how to reconceptualize work and retirement. It is particularly unsatisfactory because it has encouraged the scapegoating of a section of the population who have in fact borne the brunt of economic recession from the 1970s onward. We would argue for a different kind of analysis to support retired people over the next few decades. It is to a discussion of this that we now turn.

Work and retirement in the twenty-first century

In this section we shall explore the kind of policies which are needed to secure the full involvement of older people in society, in a range of work, work-related and non-work roles. First, however, some general points need to be made about the principles around which an alternative policy needs to be developed. A starting-point must be the observation that even if we accept the argument that demographic change and the shortage of younger workers demands a change in early exit patterns, then certain conditions need to be established before we encourage a reversal of current trends. Some examples of the principles we need to adopt have been identified by Malcolm Morrison (1986), where he assesses the new social consensus and pattern of obligations that will need to be developed to diminish the possibility of tensions between generations. Morrison argues that first, we shall need new social values which emphasize the need for productive contributions by older people. In other words, it is insufficient to say simply that we must encourage more older people to delay their retirement or to come back into the work-force; instead, critical questions must be asked about the roles that older people are allowed to play in society. In short, it is not just older people who should be asked to change; work and work-related institutions may themselves have to adapt (given the evidence cited in Chapter 3) to the realities of an ageing population.

Part of this change, Morrison argues, must also revolve around abandoning the traditional work/retirement dichotomy. Instead, we should

place a higher social value on using the creativity, talent and motivation of people throughout their lives. This broad social goal can be achieved by adopting the concept of work–retirement continuum that involves lifelong education and training. Only then will the definition of retirement gradually change, will public and private policies be modified to bring about a society that offers innovative alternatives for work and retirement, and will there be major enhancement of the roles and responsibilities of older persons.

(Morrison 1986: 363)

This broader debate is an essential starting-point for working through the implications of early exit. What needs to be recognized is that the debate about early retirement, welfare generations or the ratio of workers to pensioners, is first and foremost not a debate about economics in any narrow sense. Instead, it concerns fundamental choices about the nature of work; who should work, for how long and in what kinds of jobs. It is clear that it is only through discussing these issues that society will clarify a role both for the early retired and reduce concerns about conflicts over resources.

Social policies for early exit

Having identified some key principles around which changes in demography and patterns of work need to be developed, we must now consider policies which can resolve some of the problems identified. These have to be seen within the context of first, the rapid and unforeseen nature of early exit; second, the diversity of routes which people take out of the labour market; third, the status ambiguity of many of those taking early exit. Essentially the task to be faced is to identify the basis for reconstructing early exit during the 1990s and beyond. However, this can be done only on the basis of the existing strengths and activities of older people. In this context, our approach to early exit must be to identify those policies which can serve to encourage different forms of interdependency. Here we would list three areas for analysis and debate:

1 Early exit, employment and the reform of pensions
2 Early exit and continuing education and training
3 Early exit and interdependency within generations.

Early exit, employment and the reform of pensions

The first task for any future policy must be to clarify rights in relation to both employment and pensions for older workers. Much of the discussion here has centred around the question of encouraging a 'decade of retirement', with the development of greater flexibility in retirement ages. However, a number of policies need to be developed alongside this reform if certain groups of workers are not to be penalized. First, there is the continuing anomaly of the different retirement ages for men and women. This situation has been criticized in a number of judgments from the European Court of Justice (ECJ). In 1986 the ECJ ruled that in the case of Helen Marshall, a Hampshire dietician, the earlier retirement age for women operated by the health authority contravened the EC Equal Treatment Directive. The Directive is not part of UK law and retirement, and pension ages are specifically excluded from our equal pay and sex discrimination legislation. Because Britain is bound by the Treaty of Rome, however, the ruling is binding on the public sector. As a result the government added an amendment to the Sex Discrimination Bill 1986 to make it unlawful for a woman to be dismissed on the grounds of age when a man of the same age would not be. A judgment in 1990, arising from the Barber versus Guardian Royal Exchange case, is having a considerable impact on pension provision. The ECJ ruling in this case was that redundancy benefits, including occupational pension rights, count as 'pay', and therefore fall under Article 119 of the EEC Treaty and the Equal Pay Directive. Private occupational schemes were deemed to fall within the contract between workers and employers, since they are without contribution by public authorities and application of the public pay principle was deemed to apply in respect of each element of remuneration in this contract. Therefore different pension ages in occupational schemes will henceforth be deemed unlawful: in short, men and women must be treated equally in occupational pension schemes.

On the basis of the influence of the above judgments it would appear likely that the confusion over pension ages will be removed in the 1990s. But there are two dangers that need to be avoided in the years ahead. First, it would be unfortunate if, in the case of occupational schemes, there was a move to a common age of 65. According to the National Association of Pension Funds, 43 per cent of its 1,200 members are in the process of eliminating discrimination though the most popular option is to move to 65 for both sexes, with only 18 per cent opting for a common age of 60. But the age of 65 is clearly both disadvantageous to women (entailing as it does a reduction in pension benefits) as well as being inconsistent with the need for flexibility, recognized on all sides of the pensions debate (Carroll 1990; Walker 1990). A second danger is that the idea of a decade of retirement is implemented, but with a lower pension for those taking retirement early in the decade and a higher pension for retirement later. The problem is if the lower pension continues through into when individuals reach their seventies and eighties, a stage at which the reduced pension could prove a major burden (with women, given their greater longevity in comparison to men, the sufferers). Michael Fogarty (1990) has suggested that it is worth exploring instead the idea of 'stepped' pensions, whether social security or occupational (see also Carroll 1990). He suggests that

> These would offer a low rate to the young old, except of course for disabled people, who will always need a full pension: then a 'normal' level of pension at, say, age 70, and possibly also a higher rate at 75 or 80.
>
> (Fogarty 1990: 10)

The problem with this idea is that it is unclear why those who choose to retire early (and who decide not to work or who cannot find work) should be discriminated against. Presumably a 'full' rather than reduced pension is desirable at any age of retirement: there is no obvious reason why the young-old are 'less deserving' than the old-old. In addition, given that many of the former are men who will almost certainly not reach the age of 75 (Indeed, one in four of men who reach 35 do not even survive to pensionable age), but who do not qualify as disabled, then a reduced pension to the 60–70-year-olds must be regarded as discriminatory against men – working-class men in particular.

The implication of these arguments is that if flexible retirement is to be introduced then this should be between the ages of 60 and 70 for both women and men. According to Walker (1990)

> This means people will be allowed to retire with full state and occupational pensions at the age of 60, if they choose to, or defer full-time employment up to the age of 70. Thus each individual in conjunction with his or her employer would have full flexibility in deciding at which point in the decade they wish to retire.
>
> (Walker 1990b: 16)

Walker goes on to make the point that retirement age will also require flexibility as regards pensions. Accordingly

> the NI Pension, SERPS and occupational pensions would be payable on retirement at the age of 60 and on grounds of age at 70. In order to avoid the inequities of the earnings rule the test of retirement at 60 would be based on number of hours worked, with 16 hours per week as the possible dividing line. A person who had ceased paid employment entirely or who worked less

than 16 hours per week would be treated as fully retired and entitled to full statutory and occupational pensions. A person who had ceased full-time employment but was continuing to work part-time (16 hours or more per week) would be treated as part-retired and be entitled to a partial pension. The person continuing in full-time employment (30 hours a week or more) would not receive any statutory pension at all.

(Schuller and Walker 1990: 16)

The case for a partial pension seems particularly strong. Here again, however, there are problems with this policy. The best-known example of a partial pension scheme is that which has operated in Sweden since 1976. Under this scheme, employees aged 60–64 can receive a partial pension if they reduce their working time by an average of at least five hours a week, and work part-time for a minimum of seventeen hours per week. In general terms the scheme has proved popular with both employers and older workers, although take-up has been sensitive to the level of the partial pension (Laczko 1988). Indeed, over the period 1976–82 more men and women aged 60–64 took partial as opposed to early retirement. A number of countries have tried to follow the Swedish model. In the last ten years such schemes have been introduced in France, the UK, Spain, Finland and the former West Germany. However, these schemes have met with only limited success. This has been the case for two main reasons: first, these countries have tried to introduce partial retirement during periods of high unemployment, whereas Sweden has had consistently full employment; second, unlike in Sweden, partial retirement schemes have tended to be run alongside attractive early retirement schemes, and this has reduced their popularity. Finally, it may also be necessary, if more employment opportunities are to be provided for older people, to consider whether there is a case for legislation in this area. In 1967 in the USA, the Age Discrimination in Employment Act (ADEA) was passed to protect older workers (aged 45–64) from a variety of discriminatory employment practices, including age-based discrimination in hiring and firing, providing employee benefits, and determining promotions, training and related areas. Amendments to the Act have now abolished mandatory retirement altogether for most categories of workers. Clearly this kind of legislation reflects a more positive stance towards older workers and their role in the labour market. However, it is important not to exaggerate the impact of the American legislation. First, the Act has made little progress in terms of reversing the trend in the USA towards earlier retirement. Second, age discrimination is still a major problem in the work-place. A survey of employers in 1981 suggested that most employers believed age discrimination was an admitted problem in many companies. Third, a major obstacle limiting the effectiveness of the ADEA is the lack of awareness on the part of the American public that the statute even exists. Individuals need to be aware of their rights if this kind of legislation is to work. However, neither government nor employers may take the kind of initiatives that would increase awareness of age discrimination in the work-place. Fourth, researchers argue that strategies aimed at protecting older workers, although increasing the job security of those who are in employment, may well intensify the problems of those who are unemployed. This is because the older workers' protected situation may make employers reluctant to hire them.

However, legislation may be important in terms of widening the opportunities available to older workers. The need for legislation has always been resisted by government and employers. But it may be important in terms of setting an agenda for change, for challenging stereotypes, and for highlighting particular areas of injustice faced by older workers. This has certainly been the view of groups which sought to draw attention to the problems of the long-term un-employed and older workers – notably the Unemployment Alliance in the 1980s and the Campaign Against Age Discrimination in Employ-ment (CAADE) in the early 1990s.

While it is important to press for legislation, we should also urge the government to implement the recommendations of the all-party House of Commons Employment Committee (House of Commons 1989). The committee recommended

1 A bi-annual report to the Commons on the progress made towards achieving 'a decade of retirement'
2 That the Employment Service should always ask employers seeking to impose age restrictions on recruitment if these are strictly necessary
3 That the government should mount a campaign with the CBI to encourage employers' awareness of the potential worth of older people and to challenge the practice of discrimination
4 A government review on its employees' retirement age and early pension entitlements to allow older people greater choice
5 A scheme for increasing the weekly 'earnings disregard' from £15 for a man and dependent wife to £60 a week for six months, to encourage the over-fifties to take on part-time work
6 That Employment Training should be opened up to unemployed people over 50 irrespective of how long they had been out of work

7 A pilot scheme which would give unemployed people over 55 £500 for an educational or training programme of their choice.

Unfortunately in the early 1990s the government continued to repeat the view that it would be neither 'practical or beneficial' to introduce age discrimination legislation, and the majority of these recommendations await implementation: notably those relating to a bi-annual report, increasing the earnings disregard and improving employment training for the over-fifties. It would still appear, therefore, that despite some initiatives jobs for older people remain a low priority (and likely to remain so given the possibility of a return to high unemployment in the 1990s).

One way of raising the profile of older workers might be to create a network of 'age discrimination officers' based in selected job centres throughout the country. They would be charged with specific tasks, such as monitoring discrimination, checking for ageism in job advertisements, creating a wider range of opportunities for older workers. Such posts would be funded by the Department of Employment but should have a consultative link with bodies such as local trades councils and chambers of commerce.

At the level of the work-place, support should be given to the section of the Institute of Personnel Management's code dealing with age discrimination. The Institute recommends the following:

1 As a general rule, age should not be used as a primary discriminator in recruitment, selection, promotion and training decisions.
2 Where age bars are used, the question should be asked 'Are they necessary and why?'
3 Organizations should consider incorporating in their equal opportunity statements their commitment not to discriminate arbitrarily on the grounds of age.
4 More should be done by organizations to provide counselling in career development and to encourage self-development for both younger and older employees.
5 Those responsible for in-house training programmes should recognize that older workers can still acquire and retain new knowledge skills.

Early exit and continuing education and training

The changes discussed in this book have brought fundamental changes to the lives of many older workers. But we must also recognize the difficulties when individuals are faced with making decisions which will influence their lives for the next twenty or more years. The problem is that while the economic system is (as we saw in Chapter 3) demanding more flexibility from older workers, support in terms of training and education remains very limited. The same might also be said in respect of preparation for those who decide to leave work, with the last national survey in this area showing that only 6 per cent of workers had access to a pre-retirement course (Coleman 1982; see also Phillipson 1981; Phillipson and Strang 1983).

The major reform we would propose here is a multi-staged approach to advice and counselling for older workers. This would involve major intervention in the life course on three occasions: at 40, 50 and 60 years. The goals on each of these occasions would be quite different. At the age of 40, we would be concerned with questions of a collective nature: what are the factors in the individual's present environment, whether at work or in the community, which are inimical to long life? We would be concerned with examining how long people had been in jobs which, on the available evidence, were deleterious to health. We would also be concerned with aspects of their social and work roles which influenced behaviour likely to cause ill-health. As Tuckett (1979) points out, we know that smoking is much more common among the working class than the middle class,

> but whether this is due to a failure to appreciate the risk of cigarette smoking or a generally low level of morale and self-esteem among people forced to undertake and adjust to dangerous, dirty and repetitive jobs, with restricted life changes, is unknown.
>
> (Tuckett 1979: 48)

Around the age of 40, therefore, there is a need for comprehensive review of 'danger points' in the individual's social environment. At this stage, however, the focus would not be on individual behaviour, but on effecting reforms both at work and in the community.

At the age of 50 it would be important to establish changes at both a collective and individual level. The treatment of middle-aged workers is still highly unsatisfactory. Manual workers face a declining income in their later years, and this inevitably creates difficulties in planning for retirement. They are also, as we have seen, vulnerable to long-term unemployment, an experience which drastically reduces any savings which have been accumulated. At age 50, therefore, a pre-retirement policy would attempt to investigate ways of maintaining (if not increasing) the individual's income up to the point of retirement. It would also need to review the implications of long-term unemployment: if it happened, how would the individual cope? What sort of resources are available to provide support? Some of these questions could be explored in the context of a 'mid-life course' organized at the worker's factory or office. The emphasis would not be on retirement as such (the area of financial planning would be the exception), but on various changes at work and in the family which although preceding retirement influenced the type of adaptation made to this period.

Finally, at age 60, a retirement course could be organized around the core elements of finance and self-help and political organization. The emphasis in both items would be on how older people – both individually and collectively – can improve the quantity and quality of resources they receive. With this type of approach courses would change from simply being a digest of information on retirement. They would, instead, become a vehicle for introducing individuals to the methods, organizations and literature which can be used to improve retirement living. The focus of the course would move from the idea that a satisfactory retirement can be achieved simply by reading the right books or even receiving the right information. Instead the underlying philosophy would be that for many individuals improvements in the standards of living will come only via a long-term process of argument and negotiation with a range of organizations and institutions within the community. The task of the pre-retirement course will be to provide the skills and confidence to meet this challenge.

Early exit and interdependency within generations

A final set of issues concerns new approaches to the question of relationships between generations, within the context of the likelihood of a continuation of trends towards early exit from work. The issues here have been somewhat clouded by the worker versus pensioner debate (see Chapter 7), with its focus on older people (the retired especially) as a dependent group in society. A major concern is the accuracy of existing notions of dependency: do they reflect the kind of role played by older people within the community? To what extent are older people still restricted by socially constructed definitions of age which fail to recognize their extensive participation in society? This point is particularly relevant in relation to the family. Cheal (1987) notes that within the system of family transfers, older people are not solely, or even largely, the recipients of economic resources. He notes American research in the 1980s which shows that in fact older people are notable providers of resources for others (to younger generations especially). Cheal comments 'It is the propensity of the elderly to give, rather than their necessity to receive, that requires sociological explanation at this time' (Cheal 1987: 141). The range of possibilities in terms of intergenerational exchange have been summarized by Jack Habib as follows:

> Children and the elderly are in themselves sources of in-kind services. As the population ages, the flow of services from these two groups potentially could increase or decrease. Looked at from another perspective, the total adult time available per child (parents plus grandparents) will rise as the population ages, as will the amount of elderly time per adult. The availability of elderly parents plus grandparents will rise as the population ages, as will the amount of elderly time per adult. The availability of elderly parents' time may constitute the enabling factor that allows their adult daughters to participate in the labour force. It has been well established that despite the decline in common intergenerational living arrangements, there is still an active exchange of assistance between the elderly and their adult children. The informal caregiving rate among the young, prime age adults, and the elderly could thus be an important element in determining the overall consequences of age structure changes for the supply of productive man-hours.
>
> (Habib 1985: 485)

The empirical evidence suggests, in fact, that older people may be reassessing the kinds of demands they can make within the family (Phillipson 1990b). The consequence of this may be to free family members to engage in sustained productive activities and for the total adult time devoted to children to increase. Both these points need to be borne in mind when the issue of intergenerational conflict is examined.

9
Reconstructing later life

Introduction

This book has identified some major changes currently affecting the working lives of older men and women. An underlying theme has been that the response to these changes has been at best half-hearted, and at worst, irrelevant to the needs of the many thousands of people affected. The response has been doubly unsatisfactory because of the way in which, by the end of the 1980s, we appeared trapped in a spiral of 'victim-blaming', with older people on the receiving end of attacks suggesting that they had become an increasing burden on the economy. The arguments for and against this view have been analysed in some detail in Chapter 8. The task we now face is to move beyond the somewhat sterile form of the discussion on generational equity. In particular, the aim of this last chapter will be to consider the question of the integration of those leaving work ahead of normal retirement age and the factors which can either assist or hinder this process.

Establishing new rites of passage

In the 1960s Marion Crawford carried out pioneering research, charting the types of life-styles which were developing among couples in retirement (Crawford 1971; 1972). One of her concerns was to examine some of the ritual behaviours associated with leaving the work-place. The question she posed was whether the retirement ritual achieves the objective associated with other such rituals, namely the smooth transition of the individual from one social status to another. Crawford (1971) made two important observations: first, she suggested that retirement rituals did have some positive effects. Thus

separation rituals 'worked' in that they did help men to transfer effectively from one social status to another, regardless of how positively or otherwise they anticipated retirement beforehand. Where the rituals were absent, the men were unable to emancipate themselves fully from the status of worker.

(Crawford 1972: 460)

Second, she noted that although the retirement ritual may have some positive effects, it 'does not obviously incorporate the individual into the next group and status' (Crawford 1972: 460). Crawford went on to suggest the case for another type of ritual:

In addition to the separation/transition rituals, therefore, there may also be a place for a ritual of incorporation. It is perhaps idealistic to hope that retiring men could be formally welcomed back, as it were, into the community as full-time members. At the risk of stigmatising them, this would at least attempt to deal with part of the problem of retirement – the losses of role and identity. Perhaps the pre-retirement courses which are being initiated in various parts of the country could eventually provide the nucleus of a ritual in which a group of retiring men and women can identify with each other and can be incorporated into the community's cohort of retired yet probably active and capable members.

(Crawford 1972: 460)

These observations are of particular relevance given the changing patterns of work described in this book. In the 1970s and 1980s a pattern of 'work-ending' evolved which was 'located at the interface between work and leisure at a point where the boundaries are less and less clearly defined. Redundancy, (early) retirement, ill-health and unemployment overlap and intermingle confusingly' (Schuller 1989: 50–1). In this situation, it is hardly surprising that the work-ender faces ambiguity in terms of his or her social status. Society, it is argued, has left them stranded in the situation of being neither worker nor pensioner: 'unemployables' with no clear designation. The response to this, following Crawford, has to be seen at two levels. First, it may be important to establish new types of rituals well ahead of normal pension age, in preparation for the changes within work which the individual is likely to face. Moreover, in a context where people may be leaving organizations where they may have been for a limited period and with whom they have a limited attachment, it is clear that rites of separation and transition may be different when contrasted with those who have worked for the same organization for thirty or more years. Such rituals may, for example, be less work-centred than those described by Crawford. They may either be family or friendship-based or have a focus within a community-setting. Moreover, unlike the rites described by Crawford, they should also include an element of incorporation into an appropriate social group. The gerontological literature suggests that the latter may develop in a number of ways. For example sociable relationships existing in middle age may continue into retirement. People may, as G. Allen and Adams (1989) point out, 'accrue as well as lose friendships at this phase of their lives'. Dorothy Jerrome (1986) has noted that a number of writers have suggested that identification with the peer group is particularly marked at certain times of life, the early years of retirement being one of them.

> In this view an old people's club might be seen as a response to liminality (the experience of being marginal and between two statuses), the need for solidarity in a state of relative deprivation and low status, and for guidelines for behaviour in socially uncharted waters.
>
> (Jerrome 1986: 348–9)

But this argument fits less well within the context of some of the changes discussed in this book. Peer group identification might be more vulnerable to processes which fragment and disunite the early retired. Included among those we have reviewed in this book are financial inequalities in mid-life (see also Hepworth and Featherstone 1982); inadequate preparation for exit from the work-force; the low status of the route 'chosen' for exit from the labour force, and lack of common identity with other people in this group.

Culture and consumption in the third age

For those taking early exit from more secure routes, it is possible to see new rites of separation, transition and incorporation beginning to emerge. For example the social integration of the early retired may be assisted by new patterns of consumption, particularly within areas such as leisure and education. This point has been discussed by Featherstone (1987) where he examines the way in which middle age is being redefined as a more youthful phase of life, one which can also extend into retirement.

> Pre-retirement planning today is presented as the management of life-style and consumption opportunities to enable retirement to be a progressive set of options and choices – a phase in which the individual is presented as still moving within the social space,

still learning, investing in cultural capital and putting off the inevitable disengagement of deep old age.

(Featherstone 1987: 134)

There is now considerable evidence for the phenomena described by Featherstone, with a substantial section of the service sector now recognizing the importance of the 50+ market for their future growth. The obvious examples here would be the specialist retirement magazines, holiday companies, the second home industry, retirement communities and private sheltered housing schemes. These are the outward trappings of a substantial group of people concerned to develop a positive life-style in the years following departure from full-time work.

The potential of older people to re-engage within the cultural and educational sphere has been examined in some detail by Peter Laslett (1989) in his book *A Fresh Map of Life*. Laslett's study is a manifesto for older people in Britain, urging them to exploit the benefits of demographic change. Thus he demonstrates that male expectation of life in Britain implies that a man who is to leave work at 55 can look forward to spending as much time in retirement as he will spend in employment after reaching his mid-thirties, twenty more years at his job and twenty years after he has left it. The corresponding figures for women are even more striking because they live longer and are expected to retire earlier. Laslett describes the implications of this:

Time, or leisure rather – and a means to use it – has ceased to be the monopoly of an elite made up of hundreds, thousands, or at most tens of thousands of persons. It is becoming a commodity of millions of our citizens, our elderly citizens, those in the Third Age. Some way, therefore, must be discovered to entrust them with our cultural future, and by the same means to relieve them of the burden of their present indolence.

(Laslett 1989: 202)

According to this perspective, those entering the third age can become the standard-bearers for cultural values which may be neglected in the second age (the period of earning and saving). There may, therefore, be at least two ways of resolving concerns about incorporating the early retired. First, to see them as entering a period where they adopt new life-styles built around new patterns of consumption; second, a broader notion of the early retired entering a period of greater personal fulfilment, with engagement in educational and cultural activities an important aspect of their lives.

At the same time, we might want to suggest that both the above types of incorporation/integration may be dependent on access to privileged sources of economic and cultural capital (a point high-lighted by Featherstone but neglected by Laslett). For those deprived of such access, two kinds of 'incorporation' are possible. The first, and gender-specific type, is for everyday life to be structured around care-tasks, initially for partners/relatives but increasingly for self (Bernard and Phillipson 1990). Such tasks are in fact a key feature of the daily lives of a substantial section of the population of older people, a fact somewhat at variance with Laslett's complaint about the 'indolence' of older people in Britain. The second type, about which more research is urgently needed, is built around the 'routinization of activities of daily living'. In other words, household maintenance and related tasks themselves become a means of assisting the individual's reintegration into a meaningful round of activities (Phillipson 1978a). But to attribute attachment to such tasks as a mark of indolence in old age is wide of the mark. Instead, we must acknowledge processes which are bound-up with a division of labour which results in privilege for some and marginalization for a near majority. This process was well summarized by Dorothy Wedderburn (1975) examining changes in the organization of and attitudes towards work in late industrial society. She argues

> From middle age onward there are emerging groups who, because of class position, the possession of technical skills in short supply, inherited wealth, or the possession of power during working life are able to extract rights which protect against redundancy and the vicissitudes of retirement. They will emerge as the relatively privileged. Others will be in marginal jobs and status, liable to lose those jobs, unable to obtain others, and with few, if any, rights to second pensions. This is what has been described as the society of unequal technocracy.
>
> (Wedderburn 1975: 241)

This book has demonstrated the accuracy of Wedderburn's view of the changing nature of work. In this context, when drawing up a balance sheet of the 1980s, the results make for largely depressing reading. First, this has been a period of missed opportunities as far as older workers and the early retired are concerned. We have failed (as outlined in Chapter 3) to change the views of employers about the value of retraining older people (although some limited initiatives can be identified). We have been unable to establish education as a right for all older people, especially those from working-class backgrounds. More generally, we have failed to develop a vision about what life in retirement could be about, given appropriate resources and imagina-tion.

At the same time, some positive signs are emerging in terms of a wider debate about the needs of groups such as older workers. This is reflected in a number of manifestos setting out the case for a fairer distribution of resources both to and within the retired population (Bornat *et al*. 1985; Schuller and Walker 1990); organizations representing older people are beginning to mount more effective campaigns, particularly in some of the areas discussed in this book (McEwan 1990); the profile of the retired is certainly being raised in discussions about ageism within the local and national media. But this book has demonstrated that there is still some way to go in terms of removing the insecurities experienced by those taking early retirement. This is an area where new policies and approaches are urgently needed. We hope that this study has made a modest contribution to this process.

References

Achenbaum, W. A. (1978). *Old Age in the New Land*. London, John Hopkins.

Addison, J. and Siebert, W. (1979). *The Market for Labour: an Analytical Treatment*. Santa Monica, Calif., Goodyear.

Adnett, N. (1989). *Labour Market Policy*. Harlow, Longman.

Allen, G. and Adams, R. (1989). 'Ageing and the structure of friendship', in R. Adams and R. Bliesner (eds) *Older Adult Friendship*. London, Sage.

Allen, S., Waton, A., Purcell, K. and Wood, S. (1986). *The Experience of Unemployment*. London, Macmillan.

Altman, R. (1982). 'Incomes of the early retired', *Journal of Social Policy* 11 : 355–64.

Arber, S. and Procter, M. (1988). *Doing Secondary Analysis*. London, Unwin Hyman.

Armstrong, D. (1983). *Political Anatomy of the Body: Medical Knowledge in Britain in the Twentieth Century*. Cambridge, Cambridge University Press.

Armstrong, P., Glyn, A. and Harrison, J. (1984). *Capitalism Since World War II*. London, Fontana.

Ashton, D. (1986). *Unemployment under Capitalism: the Sociology of British and American Labour Markets*. Brighton, Wheatsheaf.

Atchley, R. (1988). *The Sociology of Retirement*. Belmont, Calif., Wadsworth.

Baboulene, B. (1976). 'The age of discrimination', *Management Today* October.

Belbin, M. (1965). *Training Methods*. Paris, OECD.

Bernard, M. and Phillipson, C. (1990). 'Self-care and health in old age', in S. Redfern (ed.) *Nursing Elderly People*. Edinburgh, Churchill Livingstone.

Berthoud, R. (1979). *Unemployed Professionals and Executives*. vol. XLV, no. 582, May, London, Policy Studies Institute.

Beveridge, W. (1944) *Full Employment in a Free Society*. London, George Allen & Unwin.

Blaikie, A. and Macnicol, J. (1986). 'Towards an anatomy of ageism: society, social policy and the elderly between the wars', in C. Phillipson, M. Bernard and P. Strang (eds) *Dependency and Dependency in Old Age*. London, Croom Helm.

Blaikie, A. and Macnicol, J. (1989). 'Ageing and social policy: a twentieth century dilemma', in A. Warnes (ed.) *Human Ageing and Later Life*. London, Edward Arnold.

Bond, J. (1986). 'Retirement: causes and consequences. Review symposium', *Ageing and Society* 6: 219–39.

Bornat, J., Phillipson, C. and Ward, S. (1985). *A Manifesto for Old Age*. London, Pluto.

Bosanquet, N. (1983). *After the New Right*. London, Heinemann.

Bosanquet, N. (1987). *A Generation in Limbo*. London, Public Policy Centre.

Bosanquet, N., Laing, W. and Propper, C. (1990). *Elderly Consumers in Britain*. London, Laing & Buisson.

Braverman, H. (1974). *Labour and Monopoly Capital*. New York, Monthly Review Press.

Brown, C. J. and Small, S. (1985).*Occupational Benefits as Social Security*. London, Policy Studies Institute.

Burgess, E. W. (ed.) (1960). *Ageing in Western Societies*. Chicago, University of Chicago Press.

Bushell, R. (1984). 'Great Britain, the job release schemes', paper produced for OECD panel, *Measures to Assist Early Retirement*. mimeo. Paris, OECD.

Butler, R. (1975). *Why Survive? Being Old in America*. New York, Harper & Row.

Bytheway, B. (1986). 'Making way: the disengagement of older workers', in C. Phillipson, M. Bernard and P. Strang (eds) *Dependency and Interdependency in Old Age-Theoretical Perspectives and Policy Alternatives*. Beckenham, Croom Helm.

Bytheway, B. (1987). 'Redundancy and the older worker', in R. Lee (ed.) *Redundancy Lay Offs and Plant Closures*. Beckenham, Croom Helm.

Calhoun, R.B. (1978). *In Search of the New Old: Redefining Old Age in America 1945–70*. New York, Elsevier.

Carroll, P. (1990). *Pension Age in a Changing Society*. London, Pension and Population Research Institute.

Casey, B. (1985). 'Early retirement schemes with a replacement condition: programmes and experiences in Belgium, France, Great Britain and the Federal Republic of Germany' *mimeo*. April 1985, Wissenschaftszentrum, Berlin.

Casey, B. and Bruche, G. (1983). *Work or Retirement? Labour Market and Social Policy for Older Workers in France, Great Britain, the Netherlands, Sweden and the USA*. Aldershot, Gower.

Casey, B. and Laczko, F. (1989). 'Early retired or long-term unemployed? The changing situation of non-working men from 1979 to 1986', *Work, Employment and Society* 3,4: 509–26.

Casey, B. and Laczko, F. (1991). 'Older worker employment in the 1990s:

some evidence from the Labour Force Survey', in G. Nigel Gilbert and R. Burrows (eds) *Fordism and Flexibility: Division and Change*. London, Macmillan.

Casey, B., Edwards, S. and Wood, S. (1989). *State Policies, Firm Policies and Early Retirement in Britain*. mimeo. London, Policy Studies Institute and London School of Economics.

CBI (1989). *Workforce 2000: An Agenda for Action*. London, Confederation of British Industry.

Chapman, S. J. and Hallsworth, H. M. (1909). *Unemployment: The Results of an Investigation made in Lancashire and an Examination of the Reports of the Poor Law Commission*. University of Manchester.

Cheal, D. (1987). 'Inter-generational transfers and life course management: towards a socio-economic perspective', in A. Bryman, B. Bytheway, P. Allatt and T. Keil (eds) *Re-Thinking the Life Cycle*. London, Macmillan.

Child Poverty Activity Group (1987). *Poverty: The Facts*. London, CPAG.

Chudacoff, H. (1989). *How Old Are You? Age Consciousness in American Culture*. Princeton, N.J., Princeton University Press.

Clark, R. and Spengler, J. (1980). *The Economics of Individual and Population Aging*. New York, Cambridge University Press.

Coleman, A. (1982). *Preparation for Retirement in England and Wales*. Leicester, National Institute of Adult Education.

Colledge, M. and Bartholomew, R. (1980). *A Study of the Long-Term Unemployed*. London, Manpower Services Commission.

Cooper, G., Cooper, R. and Eaker, L. (1988). *Living with Stress*. Harmondsworth, Penguin.

Coulson-Thomas, C. (1990). *Too Old at 40?* London, British Institute of Management.

Cowgill, D. O. (1974). 'The ageing of populations and societies', *Annals of the American Academy for Political and Social Science* 415: 1–18.

Cowgill, D. O. and Holmes, D. (eds) (1972). *Ageing and Modernisation*, New York, Appleton-Century-Crofts.

Crawford, M. (1971). 'Retirement and disengagement', *Human Relations* 24: 255–78.

Crawford, M. (1972). 'Retirement: a rite de passage', *Sociology* 6: 477–61.

Creigh, S., Roberts, C., Gorman, A. and Sawyer, P. (1986). 'Self-employment in Great Britain', *Employment Gazette* 93,9: 183–94.

Dale, A. and Bamford, C. (1988). 'Older workers and the peripheral workforce: the erosion of gender differences', *Ageing and Society* 8, 1: 43–62.

Dale, A. and Glover, J. (1989). 'Women at work in Europe', *Employment Gazette* 97, 6: 299–308.

Dale, A., Arber, S. and Procter, M. (1988). *Doing Secondary Analysis*. London, Unwin Hyman.

Daniel, W. W. (1972). *Whatever Happened to the Workers of Woolwich?* London, Political and Economic Planning.

Daniel, W. W. (1974). *A National Survey of the Unemployed*, October, London, Political and Economic Planning.

Daniel, W. W. and Stilgoe, E. (1977). *Where are They Now? A Follow-up Study of the Unemployed*. November, London, Political and Economic Planning.

Daniel, W. W. and Stilgoe, E. (1978). *The Impact of Employment Protection Laws*. London, Policy Studies Institute.

Davidoff, L. and Hall, C. (1987). *Family Fortunes: Men and Women of the English Middle Class 1780–1850*. London, Hutchinson.

Deem, R. (1986). *All Work and No Play: The Sociology of Women and Leisure*. Milton Keynes, Open University Press.

Department of Employment (1970). *Ryhope: A Pit Closes*. London, HMSO.

Department of Employment (1978). 'Measures to alleviate unemployment in the medium term: early retirement', *Employment Gazette* March: 283–5.

Department of Employment (1980). 'The job release scheme', *Employment Gazette* 88, 7: 720–26.

Department of Employment (1989). 'Labour force outlook to the year 2000', *Employment Gazette* April: 159–72.

Department of Health and Social Security (1976). *Priorities for Health and Personal Social Services*. London, HMSO.

Department of Health and Social Security (1978). *A Happier Old Age*. London, HMSO.

Department of Health and Social Security (1981a). Evidence to House of Commons Social Services Committee, Third Report from the Social Services Committee, Session 1981–82, Age of Retirement, vol. II. London, House of Commons, Paper 26–II.

Department of Health and Social Security (1981b). *Growing Older*, Cmnd 8173. London. HMSO.

Department of Health and Social Security (1985a). *Reform of Social Security: Programme for Change*, vol. 2, Cmnd 9518. London, HMSO.

Department of Health and Social Security (1985b). *Reform of Social Security: Background Papers*, vol. 3, Cmnd 9519. London, HMSO.

Department of Social Security (1990). *Retiring? Your Pension and Other Benefits*. London, HMSO.

Dex, S. (1985). *The Sexual Divisions of Work*. Brighton, Wheatsheaf.

Dex, S. (1989). 'Gender and the labour market', in D. Gallie (ed.) *Employment in Britain*. Oxford, Basil Blackwell.

Dex, S. and Phillipson, C. (1986). 'Social policy and the older worker', in C. Phillipson and A. Walker (eds) *Ageing and Social Policy: A Critical Assessment*. Aldershot, Gower.

Doering, M., Rhodes, R. S. and Schuster, M. (1983). *The Aging Worker: Research and Recommendations*. London/Beverly Hills, Calif., Sage.

Doeringer, P. B. and Piore, M. J. (1971). *Internal Labour Markets and Manpower Analysis*. Lexington, Mass., D.C. Heath.

Donaldson, A. (1979). *The British Unemployment Figures in Context*. Berlin, International Institute of Management.

Employment Committee (1989). *The Employment Patterns of the Over 50s*. Report of the House of Commons Employment Committee, Session 1988–89. London, HMSO.

Equal Opportunities Commission (1989). 'Age discrimination: over the hill at 45?' *Equal Opportunities Review* no. 25, May/June.

Ermisch, J. (1982). 'Resources of the elderly-impact of established conditions and present trends', in M. Fogarty (ed.) *Retirement Policy: The Next Fifty Years*. London, Heinemann.

Ermisch, J. (1990). *Fewer Babies, Longer Lives*. York, Joseph Rowntree Foundation.

Esping-Andersen, G. (1990). *The Three Worlds of Welfare Capitalism*. Cambridge, Polity.

Estes, C., Swan, C. L. and Gerard, L. (1982). 'Dominant and competing paradigms in gerontology: towards a political economy of old age', *Ageing and Society* 2: 151–64.

European Commission (1987). *Old Age Pensions: Net Benefits Compared to Previous Net Earnings*, vol. A. Overall Report. Brussels, Commission of the European Communities.

Falkingham, J. (1989). 'Dependency and ageing in Britain: a re-examination of the evidence', *Journal of Social Policy* 18, part 2: 211–34.

Featherstone, M. (1987). 'Leisure, symbolic power and the life course', in J. Horne, D. Jary and A. Tomlinson (eds) *Sport, Leisure and Social Relation*. Sociological Review Monograph no. 33.

Featherstone, M. and Hepworth, M. (1989). 'Ageing and old age: reflections on the postmodern life course', in B. Bytheway, T. Keil, P. Allatt and A. Bryman (eds) *Becoming and Being Old: Sociological Approaches to Later Life*. London, Sage.

Feldman, J. J. (1983). 'Work ability of the aged under conditions of improving mortality', *Health and Society* 61: 431-43.

Fennell, G., Phillipson, C. and Evers, H. (1988). *The Sociology of Old Age*. Milton Keynes, Open University Press.

Fischer, D. H. (1977). *Growing Old in America*. New York, Oxford University Press.

Fogarty, M. (1975). *40 to 60: How We Waste the Middle Aged*. London, Centre for Studies in Social Policy/Bedford Square Press.

Fogarty, M. (ed.) (1982). *Retirement Policy: The Next Fifty Years*. London, Heinemann.

Fogarty, M. (1990). *The Role of Personal and Occupational Pensions in Retirement*, Resource Paper EE4, London, Age Concern.

Foner, N. (1984). *Ages in Conflict*. New York, Columbia University Press.

Forssman, S. (1972). 'The aging worker in industrialized society', in J. Fry (ed.) *Industrial Democracy and Labour Market Policy in Sweden*. Oxford, Pergamon Press.

Friedmann, E. and Adamchak, D. (1983). 'Societal aging and inter-generational support systems', in A. M. Guillemard (ed.) *Old Age and the Welfare State*. London, Sage.

Fry, V., Smith, S. and White, S. (1990). *Pensioners and the Public Purse*. London, Institute of Fiscal Studies.

Gallup (1990). *Ageism: The Problem of the 1990s*. Report for Brook Street Employment Bureau, London.

Gaullier, X. (1982). 'Economic crisis and old age: old age policies in France', *Ageing and Society* 2: 165–82.

Gaullier, X. (1988a). 'What future for older workers', Report IV, EEC Colloquium of *Ageing and the Working Population*, Brussels.

Gaullier, X. (1988b). *La deuxieme carriere*, Editions du Seuil, Paris.

Glyn, A. and Sutcliffe, B. (1972). *British Capitalism, Workers and the Profits Squeeze*. Harmondsworth, Penguin.

Glyptis, S. (1989). *Leisure and Unemployment*. Milton Keynes, Open University Press.

Goldthorpe, J. (1984). 'The end of convergence: corporatist and dualist tendencies in modern western societies', in J. Goldthorpe (ed.) *Order and Conflict in Contemporary Capitalism*. Oxford, Clarendon Press.

Government Actuary (1979). *Occupational Pension Schemes*. Government Actuary, Fifth Survey. London, HMSO.

Graebner, W. (1980). *A History of Retirement*. New Haven, Conn., Yale University Press.

Griew, S. (1964). *Job Re-design*. Paris, OECD.

Guillemard, A. (1989). 'The trend towards early labour force withdrawal and the reorganisation of the life course: a cross-national analysis', in P. Johnson, C. Conrad, D. Thomson (eds) *Workers Versus Pensioners: Intergenerational Justice in an Ageing World*, Manchester University Press.

Haber, C. (1978). 'Mandatory retirement in nineteenth century America', *Journal of Social History* 12, part 1: 77–96.

Habib, J. (1985). 'The economy and the aged', in R. Binstock and Shanas E. (eds) *Handbook of Aging and the Social Sciences*. New York, Van Nostrand, Reinhold.

Hakim, C. (1989). 'Workforce restructuring, social insurance coverage and the black economy', *Journal of Social Policy* 18, 4: 471–503.

Ham, C. and Hill, M. (1984). *The Policy Process in the Modern Capitalist State*. London, Wheatsheaf Books.

Hanawalt, B. (1986). *The Ties that Bound*. Oxford, Oxford University Press.

Hannah, L. (1986). *Inventing Retirement*, Cambridge, Cambridge University Press.

Harper, S. and Thane, P. (1989). 'The consolidation of old age as a phase in life, 1945–1965', in M. Jeffries (ed.) *Growing Old in the Twentieth Century*. London, Routledge.

Harvey, D. (1989). *The Condition of Postmodernity*. Oxford, Basil Blackwell.

Hedstrom, P. and Ringen, S. (1987). 'Age and income in contemporary society: a research note', *Journal of Social Policy* 16, 2: 227–39.

Hendricks, J. and McAllister, C. (1983). 'An alternative perspective in retirement: a dual economic approach', *Ageing and Society* 3: 297–301.

Hepworth, M. and Featherstone, M. (1982). *Surviving Middle Age*. Oxford, Basil Blackwell.

Heron, A. and Chown, S. M. (1967). *Age and Function*. London, Churchill.

House of Commons (1982). *Third Report from the Social Services Committee*, Session 1981–82, Age of Retirement, London, House of Commons.

House of Commons (1989). Employment Committee (Second Report) *The Employment Patterns of the Over-50s*, vol. 11, London, House of Commons.

Hunt, A. (1978). *The Elderly at Home: A Study of People Aged Sixty-Five and Older Living in the Community in England in 1976*. London, HMSO.

Hunt, A. (ed.) (1988). *Women and Paid Work: Issues of Equality*. London, Macmillan.

Institute of Manpower Studies (1983). *Early Retirement*. Brighton, IMS.

Institute of Manpower Studies (1987). *Patterns of Retirement*. Brighton, IMS.

International Labour Organization (1979). *Older Workers: Work and Retirement*. Geneva, ILO.

International Labour Organization (1989). *From Pyramid to Pillar – Population Change and Social Security in Europe*. London, ILO.

Jacobs, K., Kohli, M. and Rein, M. (1987). *Testing the Industry-Mix Hypothesis of Early Exit*. Discussion paper IIVG/87-229. Berlin, Wissenschaftszentrum.

Jacobs, K. and Rein, M. (1988). *The Future of Early Retirement*, Working Paper Series. Berlin, Science Centre.

Jackson, M. (1984). 'Early retirement: recent trends and implications', *Industrial Relations Journal* 15, 3 : 21–8.

Jerrome, D. (1986). 'Me Darby, You Joan', in C. Phillipson, M. Bernard and P. Strang (eds) *Dependency and Inter-Dependency in Later Life*. Beckenham, Croom Helm.

Johnson, P. (1989a). 'The structured dependency of the elderly: a critical note', in M. Jeffries (ed.) *Growing Old in the Twentieth Century*. London, Routledge.

Johnson, P. (1989b). 'Old age creeps up', *Marxism Today* January: 34–9.

Johnson, P., Conrad, C. and Thomson, D. (eds) (1989). *Workers Versus Pensioners: Intergenerational Justice in An Ageing World*. Manchester University Press in association with the Centre for Economic Policy Research.

Jolly, J., Creigh, S. and Mingay, A. (1980). *Age as a Factor in Employment*. Research Paper no. 11, London, Department of Employment.

de Jouvenel, H. (1989). *Europe's Ageing Population. Trends and Challenges to 2025*. Guildford, Butterworth.

King, G. B. and Stearns, P. (1981). 'The retirement experience as a policy factor', *Journal of Social History* 14, 4: 589–625.

Kohli, M. (1986). 'The world we forgot: a historical review of the life course', in V. W. Marshall (ed.) *Later Life: The Social Psychology of Aging*. Beverly Hills, Calif., Sage.

Kohli, M. (1988). 'Ageing as a challenge for sociological theory', *Ageing and Society* 8, 367–94. Cambridge University Press.

Kohli, M., Rein, M., Guillemard, A. M. and Gunsteren, H. (1991). *Time for Retirement*. New York, Cambridge University Press.

Labour Force Survey (1985). *The Labour Force Survey*. OPCS, London, HMSO.

Lacroix, T. and Gruergoat, C. J. (1984). 'Le succés des pré retraites a permis de stabiliser le chômage', *Dossiers Statistiques du Travail et de L'Emploi* no.3–4, juin 1984, INSEE, Paris.

Laczko, F. (1986). *Early Retirement: An Overview of Policies in OECD Countries*, Report for OECD, mimeo, Paris, OECD.

Laczko, F. (1987). 'Older workers, unemployment and the discouraged worker effect', in S. Di Gregorio (ed.) *Social Gerontology: New Directions*. London, Croom Helm.

Laczko, F. (1988). 'Partial retirement: an alternative to early retirement? A comparison of phased retirement schemes in the United Kingdom, France and Scandinavia', *International Social Security Review* XLI, 2: 149–70.

Laczko, F. (1989). 'Between work and retirement: becoming "Old" in the 1980s', in B. Bytheway, T. Keil, P. Allatt and A. Bryman (eds) *Becoming and Being Old: Sociological Approaches to Later Life*. London, Sage.

Laczko, F. (1990). 'New poverty and the old poor: pensioners' incomes in the European Community', *Ageing and Society* 10: 261–77.

Laczko, F. (1990). 'Early exit and the employment of older workers in the 1990s', in J. Habib and C. Nusberg (eds) *Worklife Options for Older Persons*. Washington, DC, International Federation on Ageing.

Laczko, F. and Phillipson, C. (1990). 'Defending the right to work', in E. McEwan (ed.) *Age: The Unrecognised Discrimination*. London, Age Concern.

Laczko, F. and Phillipson, C. (forthcoming). 'Great Britain: the contradictions of early exit', in M. Kohli, M. Rein, A. Guillemard and H. Van Gunsteren (eds) *Time for Retirement*. New York, Cambridge University Press.

Laczko, F. and Walker, A. (1985), 'Excluding older workers from the labour market: early retirement policies in Britain, France and Sweden', in C. Jones and M. Brenton (eds) *The Year Book of Social Policy in Britain 1984–85*. London, Routledge & Kegan Paul.

Laczko, F., Dale, A., Arber, S. and Gilbert, N. (1988). 'Early retirement in a period of high unemployment', *Journal of Social Policy* 17, 2: 313–34.

Laslett, P. (1989). *A Fresh Map of Life*. London, Weidenfeld & Nicolson.

LMQR (1986). *Labour Market Quarterly Report*. July, Sheffield, Manpower Services Commission.

Long, J. (1987). 'Continuity as a basis for change: leisure and male retirement', *Leisure Studies* 6: 55–70.

Long, J. (1989). 'A part to play: men experiencing leisure through retirement', in B. Bytheway, T. Keil, P. Allatt and B. Bryman (eds) *Being and Becoming Old: Sociological Approaches to Later Life*. London, Sage.

McDonald, E. G. (1928). 'When a man wears out', *Factory and Industrial Management* 75: 536–8.

McEwan, E. (ed.) (1990). *Age: The Unrecognised Discrimination*. London, Age Concern.

McGoldrick, A. (1982). 'Early retirement: a double-edged strategy', paper presented to British Society of Gerontology Conference, Old Age in a Changing Society, September, mimeo, Exeter.

McGoldrick, A. (1983). 'Company early retirement schemes and private pension options: scope for leisure and new life styles', *Leisure Studies* 2: 187–202.

McGoldrick, A. (1984). *Equal Treatment in Occupational Pension Schemes*. Manchester, Equal Opportunities Commission.

McGoldrick, A. and Cooper, C. (1980). 'Voluntary early retirement: taking the decision', *Employment Gazette* August: 859–64.

McGoldrick, A. and Cooper, C. (1989). *Early Retirement*. Aldershot, Gower.

MacKay, D. I. (1973). 'Redundancy and re-engagement: a study of car workers', Manchester School, September.

Makeham, P. (1980). *Economic Aspects of the Employment of Older Workers*. Research Paper no. 14. London, Department of Employment.

Makeham, P. and Morgan, S. (1980). *Evaluation of the Job Release Scheme*, Research Paper no. 14. London, Department of Employment.

Markides, K. and Cooper, C. (eds) (1987). *Retirement in Industrialised Societies*. London, John Wiley.

Martin, J. and Fryer, R. H. (1973). *Redundancy and Paternalist Capitalism*. London, Allen & Unwin.

Martin, J. and Roberts, C. (1984). *Women and Employment: A Lifetime Perspective*, Social Survey Report SS1143. London, HMSO.

Miller, M. (1982). 'The development of occupational pension schemes in Britain between 1936 and 1979', unpublished typescript, University of Bath, October.

Ministry of Labour Gazette (1967). 'Forecasts of the working population 1961–1981', LXXIV: 718–20. London, HMSO.

Ministry of Labour and National Service (1953). *Annual Report, 1952*, Cmnd 8893. London, HMSO.

Ministry of Labour and National Service (1959). *Annual Report, 1958*, Cmnd 745. London, HMSO.

Ministry of Pensions and National Insurance Report (1954). *Reasons Given for Retiring or Continuing at Work*. London, HMSO.

Morrison, M. (1986). 'Work and retirement in an older society', in A. Pifer and L. Bronte (eds) *Our Aging Society*. London, W. W. Norton.

Myles, J. (1984). *Old Age in the Welfare State*. Boston, Mass., Little, Brown.

National Advisory Committee on the Employment of Older Men and Women (1953). *First Report*, Cmnd. 8963. London, HMSO.

National Advisory Committee on the Employment of Older Men and Women (1955). *Second Report*, Cmnd. 9262. London, HMSO.

National Carers Survey (1990). *Care to Work*, vol. 1 (Survey Report). London, Opportunities for Women.

National Economic Development Office (1988). 'Young people and the labour market', *A Challenge for the 1990s*. London, NEDO/Training Commission.

National Economic Development Office (1989). *Defusing the Demographic Time Bomb*. London, NEDO.

Neugarten, B. and Neugarten, D. (1986). 'Changing meanings of age in the aging society', in A. Pifer and L. Bronte (eds), *Our Aging Society: Paradox and Promise*. Ontario, Norton.

OECD (1988a). *Employment Outlook*. Paris, OECD.

OECD (1988b). *Ageing Populations: The Social Policy Implications*. Paris, OECD.

OECD (1989). *The Future of Social Protection*. Paris, OECD.

Offe, C. (1984). *Contradictions of the Welfare State*. London, Hutchinson.

O'Higgins, M. (1986). 'Public/private interaction and pension provision' in M. Rein and L. Rainwater (eds) *Public/Private Interplay in Social Protection*. M. E. Sharpe, Inc., New York, Chapter 4.

OPCS (1986). *The Labour Force Survey 1983 and 1984*. London, HMSO.

Palmer, J. and Gould, S. (1986). 'Economic consequences of population aging', in A. Pifer and L. Bronte (eds) *Our Aging Society: Paradox and Promise*. Ontario, Norton.

Palmore, B., Burchett, B., Fillenbaum, C., George, L. and Wallman, L. (1985). *Retirement: Causes and Consequences*, New York, Springer.

Parker, S. (1980). *Older Workers and Retirement*. OPCS, London, HMSO.

Parker, S. (1982). *Work and Retirement*. London, George Allen & Unwin.

Parker, S., Thomas, C. G., Ellis, N. D. and McCarthy, W. E. J. (1971). *Effects of the Redundancy Payments Act*. London, HMSO.

Parnes, H. and Less, L. (1984). 'From work to retirement: the experience of a national sample of men', *mimeo*. Ohio State University, Centre for Human Resource Research.

Parsons, T. (1942). 'Age and sex in the structure of the United States', *American Sociological Review* 7: 604–16.

Phillips Report (1954). *Report of the Committee on the Economic and Financial Problems of the Provision for Old Age*, Cmd 933. London, HMSO.

Phillipson, C. (1977). *The Emergence of Retirement*. University of Durham, Working Papers in Sociology, no. 14. Durham University Press.

Phillipson, C. (1978). 'The experience of retirement: a sociological analysis', Ph.D. thesis, University of Durham.

Phillipson, C. (1981). 'Pre-retirement education: the British and American Experience', *Ageing and Society* 3: 393–413.

Phillipson, C. (1982). *Capitalism and the Construction of Old Age*. London, Macmillan.

Phillipson, C. (1987). 'The transition to retirement', in G. Cohen (ed.) *Social Change and the Life Course*. London, Tavistock.

Phillipson, C. (1990a). 'The sociology of retirement', in J. Bond and P. Coleman (eds) *Ageing and Society: An Introduction to Social Gerontology*. London, Sage.

Phillipson, C. (1990b). *Delivering Community Care Services for Older People: Problems and Prospects for the 1990s*, Working Paper no 3, Centre for Social Gerontology, Keele, University of Keele.

Phillipson, C. (1991). 'Inter-generational relations: conflict or consensus in the twentieth century, *Policy and Politics* 19, 1: 27–36.

Phillipson, C. and Strang, P. (1983). *Pre-Retirement Education: A Longitudinal Evaluation.* Stoke-on-Trent, Department of Adult Education, University of Keele.

Phillipson, C. and Walker, A. (eds) (1986). *Ageing and Social Policy.* Aldershot, Gower.

Phillipson, C. and Walker, A. (1987). 'The case for a critical gerontology', in S. di Gregorio (ed.) *Social Gerontology: New Directions.* London, Croom Helm.

Piachaud, D. (1986). 'Disability, retirement and unemployment of older men', *Journal of Social Policy* 15, 2: 145–62.

Pifer, A. and Bronte, L. (eds) (1986). *Our Aging Society: Paradox and Promise.* Ontario, Norton.

Pilch, M. and Carroll, B. (1977). *State Pension Ages – Flexibility: the key to Equality?* Noble Lowndes, Division of Lowndes Lambert Group.

Pilgrim Trust (1938). *Men Without Work.* Cambridge.

Piore, M. J. (1975). 'Notes for a theory of labour market stratification', in R. Edwards, M. Reich and D. Gordon (eds) *Labour Market Segmentation.* Lexington, Mass., D.C. Heath.

Preston, S. (1984). 'Children and the elderly: divergent paths for America's dependents', *Demography* XXI, 435–57.

Ragot, M. (1985). 'La cessation anticipée d'activité salariée', *Conseil Economique et Social, Journal Officiel* Octobre, 26 rue Desaix, Paris, 75015.

Richardson, J. H. (1936). *Industrial Employment and Unemployment in West Yorkshire.* London, Allen & Unwin.

Ritchie, J. and Barrowclough, R. (1983). *Paying for Equalisation.* Manchester, Equal Opportunities Commission.

Robin, J. (1984). 'Family care of the elderly in a nineteenth century Devonshire parish', *Ageing and Society* 4: 505–16.

Rowntree, B. S. (1947). *Old People: Report of a Survey Committee.* Oxford, Oxford University Press.

Rowntree, B. S. and Lasker, B. (1911). *Unemployment: A Social Study.* London, Macmillan.

Royal Commission on Population (1949). *Report.* London, HMSO.

Schuller, T. (1987). 'Second adolescence? The transition from paid employment', *Work, Employment and Society* 1: 352–70.

Schuller, T. (1989). 'Work-ending: employment and ambiguity in later life' in B. Bytheway, T. Keil, P. Allatt and A. Bryman (eds) *Becoming and Being Old: Sociological Approaches to Later Life.* London, Sage.

Schuller, T. and Walker, A. (1990). *The Time of Our Life.* London, Institute for Public Policy Research.

Schulz, J. H. (1980). *The Economics of Ageing,* Belmont, Calif., Wadsworth.

Shanas, E., Townsend, P., Wedderburn, D., Friis, H., Milhoj, P. and Stehouwer, J. (1968). *Old People in Three Industrial Societies.* London, Routledge & Kegan Paul.

Shrank, H. and Waring, J. (1989). 'Older workers: ambivalence and interventions', *Annals of the American Academy of Political and Social Science* 503: 113–27.

Sinfield, A. (1976). 'Unemployment and social structure', in N. Worswick (ed.) *The Concept and Measurement of Involuntary Unemployment*. London, Allen & Unwin.

Slater, R. (1973). 'Age discrimination', *New Society* 10 May: 301–2.

Slater, R. and Kingsley, S. (1976). 'Predicting age-prejudiced employers: a British pilot study, *Industrial Gerontology* Spring, 138–49.

Smith, R. (1984). 'The structured dependence of the elderly in the Middle Ages and thereafter', *Ageing and Society* 4, part 4: 409–28.

Sokolovsky, J. (ed.) (1983). *Growing Old in Different Societies*. Belmont, Calif., Wadsworth.

Spence, A. (1990). 'Labour force outlook to 2001', *Employment Gazette* 98.4: 186–98.

Standing, G. (1986). 'Labour flexibility and older worker marginalisation: the need for a new strategy', in *International Labour Review* 125, 3: 329–45.

Stearns, P. (1975). *Lives of Labour*. London, Croom Helm.

Stearns, P. (1977). *Old Age in European Society: The Case of France*. London, Croom Helm.

Stevenson, J. and Cook, C. (1977). *The Slump: Society and Politics During the Depression*. London, CAPE.

Stone, R. and Minkler, M. (1984). 'The socio-political context of women's retirement', in M. Minkler, and C. Estes (eds) *Political Economy of Ageing* Baywood, New York, 225–38.

Survey Committee of Barnett House (1938). *A Survey of the Social Services in the Oxford Area*. Oxford.

Thane, P. (1978). 'The muddled history of retiring at 60 and 65', *New Society* 3 August: 234–6.

Thane, P. and Harper, S. (1989). 'The consolidation of old age as a phase of life 1945–1965', in M. Jefferys (ed.) *Growing Old in the Twentieth Century*. London, Routledge.

Thomas, K. (1976). 'Age and authority in early modern England', *Proceedings of the British Academy* LXII: 205–48.

Thompson, D. (1989). 'The welfare state and generational conflict: winners and losers', in P. Johnson, C. Conrad, and D. Thompson (eds) *Workers Versus Pensioners*. Manchester University Press in association with the Centre for Economic Policy Research.

Thompson, P. (1989). *The Nature of Work*, 2nd edn. London, Macmillan.

Townsend, P. (1979). *Poverty in the United Kingdom*. Harmondsworth, Pelican.

Townsend, P. (1981). 'The structured dependency of the elderly', *Ageing and Society* 1: 5–28.

Townsend, P. (1986). 'Ageism and social policy', in C. Phillipson and A. Walker (eds) *Ageing and Social Policy: A Critical Assessment*. Aldershot, Gower.

Townsend, P. and Wedderburn, D. (1965). *The Aged in the Welfare State*. London, Bell.

Tracey, M. (1979). *Retirement Age Practices in Ten Industrial Societies, 1960–1976*. Geneva, International Social Security Association.

Tuckett, (1979). 'Choices for health education: a sociological view', in D. Sutherland (ed.) *Health Education: Perspectives and Choices*. London, Allen & Unwin.

Varlaam, C. and Bevan, S. (1987). *Patterns of Retirement*. Institute of Manpower Studies, Report no. 134. University of Sussex.

Verbrugge, L. M. (1984). 'Longer life but worsening health? Trends in mortality of middle-aged and older persons', *Milbank Memorial Fund Quarterly* 62: 616–19.

Walker, A. (1981). 'Towards a political economy of old age', *Ageing and Society* 1, part 1: 73–94.

Walker, A. (1986). 'Pensions and the production of poverty in old age', in C. Phillipson, and A. Walker *Ageing and Social Policy*. Aldershot, Gower.

Walker, A. (1989). 'The social division of early retirement', in M. Jefferys (ed.) *Growing Old in the Twentieth Century*. London, Routledge

Walker, A. (1990a). 'The benefits of old age?: age discrimination and social security', in E. McEwen (ed.) *Age the Unrecognised Discrimination*. London, Age Concern.

Walker, A. (1990b). 'A flexible decade of retirement', in T. Schuller and A. Walker *The Time of Our Life*. London, Institute for Public Policy Research.

Walker, A. and Laczko, F. (1982). 'Early retirement and flexible retirement', in House of Commons Social Services Committee, *Age of Retirement*, HC26–11. London, HMSO.

Walker, A., Noble, I. and Westergaard, J. (1985). 'From secure employment to labour market insecurity: the impact of redundancy on older workers in the steel industry', in B. Roberts, R. Finnegan and D. Gallie (eds) *New Approaches to Economic Life*. Manchester University Press.

Wedderburn, D. (1975). 'Prospects for the reorganisation of work', *Gerontologist* June: 236–41.

Welford, A. T. (1958). *Ageing and Human Skill*. London, Oxford University Press for the Nuffield Foundation.

Welford, A. T. (1976). 'Thirty years of psychological research on age and work', *Journal of Occupational Psychology* 49: 129–38.

Wells, B. (1989). 'The labour market for young and older workers', *Employment Gazette* June: 319–31.

West, P., Illsley, R. and Kelman, K. (1984). 'Public preference for the care of dependency groups', *Social Science and Medicine* 18, 4: 287–95.

Westergaard, J., Noble, I. and Walker, A. (1988). *After Retirement: The Experience of Insecurity*. Oxford, Polity Press.

White, M. (1980). *Shorter Working Time*. London, Policy Studies Institute.

White, M. (1983). *Long-Term Unemployment and Labour Markets*. London, Policy Studies Institute.

Whitehead, M. (1989). *Inequalitites in Health: The Black Report and the Health Divide*. London, Penguin.

Willis, P. (1977). *Learning to Labour*. Farnborough, Saxon House.

Wood, S. (1980). 'Managerial reactions to job redundancy through early retirement', *Sociological Review* 28, 4: 783–807.

Wright, F. (1986). *Left to Care Alone*. Aldershot, Gower.

Index

Achenbaum, W. A., 16
Adnett, N., 39
Advisory Committee on the Employ-
    ment of Older men and Women, 28,
    36
Age Concern, 99
age discrimination, 8, 14, 16–17, 28–45,
    65, 119–20
    Institute of Personnel Management
        code, 121
    officers to combat, 121
    in public sector, 32, 34
    and recruitment, 31–3
    and women, 33
Age Discrimination in Employment Act
    (ADEA) (US), 119–20
age-performance relationship, 35–7
ageing,
    political economy of, 3–5
    'reconstruction' of, 3
ageism see age discrimination
Altman, R., 66–7, 75
Arber, S., 50, 53, 61, 62, 65, 71, 73, 75,
    79, 82
Ashton, D., 35
Atchley, R., 13, 29
Australia, 59
Austria, 91, 107

Bamford, C., 40–1
Barber v. Guardian Royal Exchange
    case, 117
Barnett House, Survey Committee, 15
Belgium, 91, 107
    Pre-pension Légale, 92–3
benefits, 50–3, 61, 73, 79, 90
    income support, 50, 79
    invalidity benefit, 52–3, 61, 73

means-tested, 50
and poverty in old age, 81
sickness benefit, 52–3, 73
supplementary benefit, 90
unemployment benefit, 50, 61, 73
working to advantage of pensioners,
    103–5
see also state retirement pension
Berthoud, R., 32–3
Birmingham Post, 16
Blaikie, A., 11–12
Bond, J., 5
Bosanquet, N., 19, 25, 30, 111
Britain, 60
    comparison of early retirement
        schemes with those in France, 91–3
    female employment patterns, 22–4
    partial pension scheme, 119
    pre-retirement movement, 29
    worker-pensioner ratio, 107
    see also Census; Job Release Scheme
        (JRS)
Buckton, Ray, 100
Burgess, E. W., 11
Bushell, R., 49, 50, 51, 71, 88, 89,
    92
Butler, Robert, 20, 29
Bytheway, B., 19, 64, 65

Campaign Against Age Discrimination
    in Employment (CAADE), 120
Canada, 59
Carroll, P., 49, 117, 118
Casey, B., 6, 7, 19, 20, 21, 23, 31, 54,
    60, 65, 71, 73, 91, 92, 111
Census of Population for England
    and Wales and for Scotland, 21,
    52–3